Amazon Connect User Guide

A catalogue record for this book is available from the Hong Kong Public Libraries.

Published in Hong Kong by Samurai Media Limited.

Email: info@samuraimedia.org

ISBN 9789888408566

Contents

Using Amazon Connect

This guide covers how to get started with using Amazon Connect to make and receive calls, generate helpful metrics and reporting, manage user permissions and security profiles, create contact flows, and scale your contact center to match your business requirements.

Amazon Connect Concepts

The terminology and concepts described below are central to your understanding and use of Amazon Connect.

instance
A container for the resources and settings of your contact center, including user directory, data encryption and storage settings, and integration settings.

Amazon Connect
The management console where configuration and reporting are managed. Each instance has a separate management console.

Contact Control Panel (CCP)
The interface through which agents handle customer contacts.

Outbound caller ID
The name and number displayed to the recipient of a call as the ID of a caller.

When you create a queue, you can specify an **Outbound caller ID name** and **Outbound caller ID number** to use for the queue. However, the information displayed to the person you call may not always match the name or number registered with the carrier for Amazon Connect. In some cases, the caller ID information is provided by the carrier of the person you are calling. The information may not be up-to-date with that carrier, or the number may get passed differently between systems due to hardware or configuration differences. If that is the case, the person you call may not see the phone number, or may see the name of a previously registered owner of the number, instead of the name of the registered person from your organization.

agent
Users who handle contacts using Amazon Connect.

users
All users of the system and web application. Users can have different roles or permissions, for example, agent, manager, or system administrator.

reports
Real-time and historical reporting for an instance, including agent activity.

status
Metrics are gathered based on changes in agent status (available, offline, and so on).

Working with User Settings

There are several roles and permissions available on Amazon Connect. The varying levels of permission allow for protection of valuable data (such as call records), and the management of resources.

Permissions also dictate which users can see various parts of Amazon Connect. For example, an agent has view-only access and is only able to see the CCP. An administrator is able to see and access all the functionality in Amazon Connect.

Managing User Profiles and Permissions

You can manage user security, routing, reporting, and contact management settings with granulated permissions and profiles.

Security Profiles

Permissions are required for users to access, view, and edit certain administrative functionality and tools. Security profiles determine which users and roles can view and perform specific tasks. The following resource groups can be edited:

- **Routing**—Routing profiles, quick connects, hours of operation, queues.
- **Numbers and flows**—Prompts, contact flows, phone numbers.
- **Users and permissions**—Users, agent grouping, security profiles, agent status.
- **Contact Control Panel (CCP)**—CCP access, outbound calls.
- **Metrics and Quality**—Access metrics, manager listen in, call recordings, saved reports.
- **Historical Changes**—View historical changes.

Security permissions for each group are further granulated to allow for different levels of permission, from allowing full read-write access to **All** resources to only allowing a user to **View** resources.

There are four default security profiles:

- **Admin**—An admin can access and edit all available resources and actions.
- **Agent**—This profile only allows access to the CCP. No other actions are available.
- **CallCenterManager**—This profile allows access to user management, metrics, and routing settings.
- **QualityAnalyst**—This profile only allows access to metrics.

To create a security profile

1. Choose **Users, Security profiles, Add new security profile**.

2. Type a name and description, and choose the appropriate permissions for each group. **Note**
   In some cases, selecting a permission results in other permissions being included. For example, if you choose **Edit**, **View** is also included.

3. Choose **Save**.

To manage and edit security profiles

1. Choose **Users, Security profiles**, and select the profile to edit.

2. Select a category name to display the options available.

3. Select or deselect options as required.

4. Choose **Save**.

To assign a security profile to a user

1. Choose **Users, User management**.

2. Select a single user (or multiple users) and choose **Edit**.

3. Select the relevant profiles from the options provided. **Note**
   If you're editing multiple users, they are all assigned the chosen settings.

4. Choose **Save**.

Routing Profiles

A routing profile is a collection of queues that determines how contacts are routed to agents. Routing profiles are used to prioritize contacts across specific queues and manage the priority in which contacts are handled based on the queues they are routed to. This can be used to ensure alignment with service SLAs. Routing profiles are managed and assigned to agents by the administrator. An agent can only be assigned a single routing profile at a time; however, they may serve multiple queues, based on rules defined in the routing profile.

To create a routing profile

1. Choose **Users**, **Routing profiles**, **Add new profile**.

2. Enter or choose the following information:

   - **Name**—A searchable display name.
   - **Description**—The routing profile's function.
   - **Routing profile queues**—A queue to associate with the routing profile. You can add multiple queues.
   - **Priority**—The order in which contacts are handled by the queue they are in. Set values in order of importance, with the lowest number equaling the highest priority. For example, a contact in a queue with a priority of 2 would be a lower priority than a contact in a queue with a priority of 1.
   - **Delay (in seconds)**—The minimum hold time before the call is routed to an agent with a matching queue/threshold combination.
   - **Default outbound queue**—Outbound calls must be associated with one of the associated queues.

3. Choose **Add new profile**.

Here's an example of a profile:

Queue	Priority	Delay (in seconds)
Premium Support 1	1	0
Premium Support 2	1	0
Premium Support 3	2	20
Premium Support 4	3	80

This profile prioritizes Premium Support 1 and Premium Support 2 equally (because each has a priority 1).

- Agents with this profile may take calls for Premium Support 3 when customers for Premium Support 3 are waiting for 20 seconds or longer (and no Premium Support 1 or Premium Support 2 calls are in queue).
- Agents with this profile may take calls for Premium Support 4 when customers for Premium Support 4 are waiting 80 seconds or longer (and no calls for Premium Support 1, Premium Support 2 or Premium Support 3 are in queue).

Understanding Contact Flows

Topics

- Contact Block Definitions
- Creating Contact Flows
- Contact Flow Logs
- Contact Flow Import/Export

A contact flow defines each step of the experience customers have when they interact with your contact center.

You can create a contact flow using the contact flow templates provided. You can also create your own contact flow from scratch, using the **Create contact flow** editor.

The following template types are available:

- **Customer queue flow**—Manages what the customer experiences while in queue, before being joined to an agent. Customer queue flows are interruptible and can include actions such as an audio clip apologizing for a delay and offering an option to receive a callback, leveraging the **Transfer to queue** block.
- **Customer hold flow**—Manages what the customer experiences while the customer is on hold. With this flow, one or more audio prompts can be played to a customer using the **Loop prompts** block while waiting on hold.
- **Customer whisper flow**—Manages what the customer experiences as part of an inbound call immediately before being joined with an agent. The agent and customer whispers are played to completion, then the two are joined.
- **Outbound whisper flow**—Manages what the customer experiences as part of an outbound call before being connected with an agent. In this flow, the customer whisper is played to completion, then the two are joined. For example, this flow can be used to enable call recordings for outbound calls with the **Set call recording behavior** block.
- **Agent hold flow**—Manages what the agent experiences when on hold with a customer. With this flow, one or more audio prompts can be played to an agent using the **Loop prompts** block while the customer is on hold.
- **Agent whisper flow**—Manages what the agent experiences as part of an inbound call immediately before being joined with a customer. The agent and customer whispers are played to completion, then the two are joined.
- **Transfer to agent flow**—Manages what the agent experiences when transferring to another agent. This type of flow is associated with transfer to agent quick connects, and often plays messaging, then completes the transfer using the **Transfer to agent** block.
- **Transfer to queue flow**—Manages what the agent experiences when transferring to another queue. This type of flow is associated with transfer to queue quick connects, and often plays messaging, then completes the transfer using the **Transfer to queue** block.

Contact Block Definitions

Contact flows are created in the contact flow editor using action blocks arranged by dragging and dropping them onto a grid. The contact flow configuration is grouped into blocks. Each group represents a specific action, and each block has editable conditions related to the group's action or behavior.

Note
When you set **User Defined** or **External** values in dynamic attribute fields, ensure that you use only alphanumeric characters (A-Z, 0–9) and periods. No other characters can be used.

Interact

Block	Action	Description
Play prompt	Plays audio.	Prompts can be an audio file, stored in the prompt library, or text-to-speech, which can optionally be specified in a flow via a contact attribute. If you use text-to-speech, you can use a maximum of 1,024 characters.
Get customer input	Branches based on customer intent.	Plays an interruptible audio prompt and branches based on DTMF or Amazon Lex intents. If you use text-to-speech, you can use a maximum of 1,024 characters. Amazon Lex bots support both spoken utterances and keypad input when used in a contact flow.
Store customer input	Stores numerical input to contact attribute.	Plays an interruptible audio prompt and stores digits via DTMF as a contact attribute. To enable encryption, contact your system administrator to add a public signing key to the **Contact flow security keys** settings of your Amazon Connect instance.
Loop prompts	Loops a sequence of prompts while a customer or agent is on hold or in queue.	When **Loop prompts** is used in a queue flow, audio playback can be interrupted with a flow at preset times.
Hold customer or agent	Places a customer or agent on or off hold.	Settings: Agent on hold / customer on call Customer on hold / agent on call Agent and customer on call

Integrate

Block	Action	Description
Invoke AWS Lambda function	Makes a call to AWS Lambda, and optionally returns key-value pairs.	The returned key-value pairs can be used to set contact attributes.

Set

Block	Action	Description
Set working queue	Specifies the queue to be used when **Transfer to queue** is invoked.	A queue must be specified before invoking **Transfer to queue**. It's also the default queue for checking attributes, such as staffing, queue status, and hours of operation. To use a Set queue block to set the queue dynamically, such as with contact attributes, you must specify the ARN for the queue rather than the queue name. To find the ARN for a queue, open the queue in the queue editor. The ARN is included as the last part of the URL displayed in the browser address bar after /queue. For example, `.../queue/76f149bd-9edb -4128-b969-347f083d1501`.
Set call recording behavior	Sets options for call recordings.	Enables or disables call recording for the agent, customer, or both.
Set contact attributes	Stores key-value pairs as contact attributes.	Contact attributes are accessible by other areas of Amazon Connect, such as the CCP and CTRs.
Get metrics	Retrieves real-time metrics about queues and agents in your contact center and returns them as attributes.	Use metrics attributes to define routing logic based on metric values, such as number of contact in a queue, number of available agents, and oldest contact in a queue. For more information, see Amazon Connect Contact Attributes
Change queue priority/routing age	Alters the priority of the contact in queue.	Routing age alters the time in queue for the contact, which determines its priority in comparison to when other contacts are received. Queue priority sets the contact to a high priority that can be compared to other contacts that have a priority set (typically between 1 and 1000).
Set hold flow	Links from one contact flow type to another.	Specifies the flow to invoke when a customer or agent is put on hold.
Set whisper flow	Overrides the default whisper by linking to a whisper flow.	Specifies the whisper to be played to customer on an outbound call, or to the customer or agent when the call is joined.

Block	Action	Description
Set callback number	Sets a callback number.	Specifies the number to be used to call the customer back in the CCP, or when **Transfer to queue** is invoked with the callback option. When specifying a phone number in Amazon Connect, the number must be in E.164 format. Numbers in E.164 format do not include the leading zeroes you would dial for a local or regional call within the same country when dialing the number from a phone. For example, if you usually dial 0400xxxxxx to place a call in Australia, the number in E.164 format includes the country code of 61 and removes the leading zero for the number. The number to use in Amazon Connect is **+61400xxxxxx**.
Set agent status	This allows for the setting of an agent status via a contact flow.	For example, you can use this with **Store customer input** to set the agent status to **On hold** so they don't hear the input from the customer during credit card entry.
Set voice	Sets the voice.	Sets the voice to interact with the customer, and optionally the voice if using text-to-speech (TTS).
Set customer queue flow	Set queue flow.	Specifies the flow to invoke when a customer is transferred to a queue.

Branch

Block	Action	Description
Check queue status	Checks the status of the queue based on specified parameters.	Branches based on the number of contacts, oldest contact in queue, or if the queue is at capacity.

Block	Action	Description
Check staffing	Checks based on whether agents are available, staffed, or online.	Branches based on whether agents are available, staffed (available, on call, and after call work), or online. You must set a queue before using a Check staffing block in your contact flow. If a queue is not set, the block always proceeds through the error branch. You can use a Set queue block to set the queue. When a contact is transferred from one flow to another, the queue that is set in a contact flow is passed from that flow to the next one.
Check hours of operation	Checks to see whether the contact is within or outside of business defined hours.	Branches based on specified hours of operation, either directly or as associated to a queue that is within open hours.
Check contact attributes	User-based comparison checks.	Branches based on a comparison to the value of a contact attribute. Examples of supported comparisons include: **Equals, Is Greater Than, Is Less Than, Starts With, Contains.**
Distribute by percentage	Routes customers randomly based on a percentage.	Like flipping a coin, contacts are distributed randomly, which doesn't guarantee exact percentage splits.

Terminate/Transfer

Block	Action	Description
Disconnect / hang up	Terminates a customer contact.	Disconnects the customer's call.
Transfer to queue	Ends the current contact flow and places the customer in queue.	A queue must be specified, using **Set queue**, before invoking **Transfer to queue**. Optionally, the contact can be placed in queue to receive a callback, if **Set customer callback number** has been invoked.

Block	Action	Description
Transfer to phone number	Transfers the customer.	Ends the current contact flow and transfers the customer to a phone number. If the country you want to select is not listed, you can submit a request to add countries you want to transfer calls to using the Amazon Connect service limits increase form.
Transfer to agent	Transfers the customer to an agent.	Ends the current contact flow and transfers the customer to an agent. If the agent is on a call, the contact is disconnected.
Transfer to flow	Transfers the customer to another flow.	Ends the current contact flow and transfers the customer to a flow of the same type, such as customer queue flow, customer hold flow, customer whisper flow, agent hold flow, agent whisper flow, transfer to agent flow, and transfer to queue flow.
End flow/return from interruption	Ends the current flow without disconnecting the caller.	This can be used to return to Loop prompts when it has been interrupted. When **End flow/return from interruption** is invoked, the customer remains connected to the system.

Creating Contact Flows

You can create a variety of contact flows in Amazon Connect, such as transfer flows and interruptible flows. The starting point for all contact flows is the contact flow editor. You can make your contact flows as simple or complex as necessary.

To create a new contact flow in Amazon Connect using the editor

1. Choose **Routing**, **Contact flows**, **Create contact flow**.

2. Type a name and a description for your contact flow.

3. Search for a block using the **Search** bar, or expand the relevant group to locate the block.

4. Drag and drop blocks onto the canvas. They don't have to be added in a specific order or sequence, as connections between the elements do not have to be strictly linear.

5. Select the block title to access the settings and editing menu.

To create connections between blocks

1. Select the originating group.

2. Select the circle for the action to perform.

3. Drag the arrow to the connector of the group that performs the next action. **Note**
   For groups that support multiple branches, drag the connector to the appropriate action.

4. Repeat the steps to create a contact flow that meets your requirements.

5. Choose **Save** to save a draft of the flow. Choose **Publish** to activate the flow immediately. **Note**
   All connectors must be connected to a block in order to successfully publish your contact flow.

A saved contact flow cannot be assigned to a number until it is published.

Contact Flow Logs

Amazon Connect contact flow logs provide you with real-time details about events in your contact flows as customers interact with them. You can use contact flow logs to help debug your contact flows as you are creating them. After you publish your contact flows, you can view the logs to gain insight into what happens during complex contact flows, and quickly identify errors that your customers encounter when they connect to your contact center.

Contact flow logs are stored in Amazon CloudWatch, in the same region as your Amazon Connect instance. A log entry added as each block in your contact flow is triggered. You can configure CloudWatch to send alerts when unexpected events occur during active contact flows. As a contact center manager, you can aggregate data from contact flow logs to analyze performance of contact flows to optimize the experience you provide for your customers. For more information about CloudWatch Logs, see the Amazon CloudWatch Logs User Guide.

Enabling Contact Flow Logs

To start generating contact flow logs, enable contact flow logs for your Amazon Connect instance. After you enable logs for your instance, logs are generated only for contact flows that include a **Set logging behavior** block with logging set to enabled. You can control which flows, or parts of flows, logs are generated for by including multiple **Set logging behavior** blocks and setting logging to enabled or disabled as desired. When you use a **Set logging behavior** block to enable or disable logging for a flow, logging is also enabled or disabled for any subsequent flow that a contact is transferred to, even if the flow does not include a **Set logging behavior** block. To avoid having logging settings persist between flows, you should include a **Set logging behavior** block in the flow with logging enabled or disabled as desired for that specific flow.

When you create a new Amazon Connect instance, you can enable Contact flow logs when you configure Data Storage settings. If you already have an Amazon Connect instance, you can enable or disable Contact flow logs for your instance in the Amazon Connect console under **Contact flow** settings. You are not charged for generating contact flow logs, but are charged for using CloudWatch for generating and storing the logs. Free tier customers are charged only for usage that exceeds service limits. For details about Amazon CloudWatch pricing, see Amazon CloudWatch Pricing.

To enable contact flow logs for your Amazon Connect instance

1. Open the Amazon Connect console.

2. Choose the instance alias for the instance for which to enable contact flow logs.

3. Choose **Contact flows**.

4. Select **Enable Contact flow logs** and choose **Apply**.

After you enable contact flow logs for your instance, you can enable logging for a flow by adding a **Set logging behavior** block.

To enable or disable contact flow logs for a contact flow

1. Add a **Set logging behavior** block and connect it to another block in the flow.

2. Open the settings for the block, and under **Logging behavior** do one of the following:

   Select **Enable** to turn on logging for the flow.

   Select **Disable** to turn off logging for the flow.

3. Choose **Save**.

4. If you add a **Set logging behavior** block to a contact flow that is already published, you must publish it again to start generating logs for it.

Data Captured in Contact Flow Logs

Log entries for contact flows include details about the block associated with the log entry, the contact ID, and the action taken after the steps in the block were completed. Any contact interaction that occurs outside of the contact flow is not logged, such as time spent in a queue or interactions with an agent. You can control which data is captured in contact flow logs by including a **Set logging behavior** block in your contact flow. You can set the properties of the block to disable logging during the parts of your contact flow that interact with or capture sensitive data or customers' personal information.

If you use Amazon Lex or AWS Lambda in your contact flows, the logs show the entry and exit of the contact flow going to them, and include any information about the interaction that is sent or received during entry or exit.

Because the logs also include the contact flow ID, and the contact flow ID stays the same when you change a contact flow, you can use the logs to compare the interactions with different versions of the contact flow.

The following example log entry shows a Set queue block of a customer queue flow.

```
1  {
2      "Timestamp": "2017-11-09T12:17.898Z",
3      "ContactId": "f0b21968-952b-47ba-b764-f29a57bcf626",
4      "ContactFlowId": "arn:aws:connect:us-east-2:0123456789012:instance/d-92673ef055/contact-flow
           /b1d791cf-1264-42e3-9a73-62cbcb3c9a45",
5      "ContactFlowModuleType": "SetQueue",
6      "Events": {
7          "Queue": [
8              "arn:aws:connect:us-east-2:670047220557:instance/d-92673ef044/queue/f0300e43
                   -9547-477c-b8ba-0bb7a72f7fa1"
9          ]
10     }
11 }
```

Tracking Customers Between Contact Flows

In many cases, customer contacts interact with multiple contact flows in your call center, being passed from one contact flow to another to appropriately assist them with their specific issue. Contact flow logs help you track customers between different contact flows, by including the ID of the contact in each log entry. When a customer is transferred to a different contact flow, the ID for the contact associated with their interaction is included with the log for the new flow. You can query the logs for the contact ID to trace the customer interaction through each contact flow. In larger, high-volume contact centers, there can be multiple streams for contact flow logs. If a contact is transferred to a different contact flow, the log may be in a different stream. To make sure that you are finding all of the log data for a specific contact, you should search for the contact ID in the entire CloudWatch log group instead of in a specific log stream.

Create Alerts for Contact Flow Log Events

You can configure CloudWatch to define a filter pattern that looks for specific events in your contact flow logs and then creates an alert when an entry for that event is added to the log. For example, you can set an alert for when a contact flow block goes down an error path as a customer interacts with the flow. Log entries are typically available in CloudWatch within a short time, giving you near real-time notification of events in contact flows.

Analyzing Contact Flow Logs with Amazon Kinesis

To perform analysis on your contact flow logs, you can set up an Amazon Kinesis stream to stream your contact flow log data from CloudWatch to a data warehouse service, such as Amazon Redshift. You can combine the contact flow log data with other Amazon Connect data in your warehouse, or run queries to identify trends or common issues with a contact flow.

Contact Flow Import/Export

You can export contact flows from and import contact flows into your Amazon Connect instance. You can use exported contact flows to create backup copies and manage version control of your contact flows. This lets you easily restore a previous version in case you encounter an error with a published contact flow. You can easily copy contact flows from one Amazon Connect instance to another, for example from a test environment to a production environment, or from one region to another as you expand your customer service organization.

Note
The Contact Flow Import/Export feature is currently in Beta status. Updates and improvements that we make could result in issues in future releases importing contact flows that are exported during the beta phase.

Because Amazon Connect contact flows are not tied to a specific instance or account, exported flows could also be imported into instances created by other customers, allowing Amazon Connect partners to create custom contact flow solutions that can be used by Amazon Connect customers.

When you export a contact flow, the most recently saved version of the flow you currently have open in the Contact Flow editor is exported as a UTF-8 encoded JSON document. Each block of your contact flow is included in the JSON document as a separate section. To import a contact flow, either one that you previous exported, or that was exported from a different Amazon Connect instance, you just select the JSON file and import it. The imported flow replaces the contact flow currently open in the editor. The imported contact flow is not added to your Amazon Connect instance until you save it after importing.

Resolving Resources in Imported Contact Flows

When you create a contact flow, the resources you include in the contact flow, such as queues and voice prompts, are referenced within the contact flow using the name of the resource and the Amazon Resource Name (ARN). The ARN is a unique identifier for a resource that is specific to the service and region in which the resource is created. When you export a contact flow, the name and ARN for each resource referenced in the contact flow is included in the exported contact flow.

When you import a contact flow, Amazon Connect attempts to resolve the references to the Amazon Connect resources used in the contact flow, such as queues, by using the ARN for the resource. When you import a contact flow into the same Amazon Connect instance that you exported it from, the resources used in the contact flow will resolve to the existing resources in that instance. If you delete a resource, or change the permissions for a resource, Amazon Connect may not be able to resolve the resource when you import the contact flow. When a resource cannot be found using the ARN, Amazon Connect attempts to resolve the resource by finding a resource with the same name as the one used in the contact flow. If no resource with the same name is found, a warning is displayed on the block that contains a reference to the unresolved resource.

If you import a contact flow into a different Amazon Connect instance than the one it was exported from, the ARNs for the resources used are different. If you create resources in the instance with the same name as the resource in the instance where the contact flow was exported from, the resources can be resolved by name. You can also open the blocks that contain unresolved resources, or resources that were resolved by name, and change the resource to another one in the Amazon Connect instance. You can save a contact flow with unresolved or missing resources, but you cannot publish it until the resources are resolved or removed.

Exporting Contact Flows

When you export a contact flow, the JSON document created for the flow includes a section for each block in the flow. The name used for a specific block, parameter, or other element of the contact flow may be different than the label used for it in the user interface (UI).

By default, contact flow export files are created without a file name extension, and saved to the default location set for your browser. We suggest saving your exported contact flows to folder that contains only exported contact flows.

Important

When you attempt to import or export a large or complex contact flow, the export may fail if the contact flow contains a large amount of blocks and resources. It may also fail if the file size for the exported contact flow exceeds 1 MB in size. An notification message is displayed when this occurs.

To export a contact flow

1. Log in to your Amazon Connect instance using an account that is assigned a security profile that includes view permissions for contact flows.

2. Choose **Routing**, **Contact flows**.

3. Open the contact flow to export.

4. Choose **Save**, **Export flow**.

5. Provide a name for the exported file, and choose **Export**.

To import a contact flow

1. Log in to your Amazon Connect instance. The account must be assigned a security profile that includes edit permissions for contact flows.

2. Choose **Routing**, **Contact flows**.

3. Do one of the following:

   - To replace an existing contact flow with the one you are importing, open the contact flow to replace.
   - Create a new contact flow of the same type as the one you are importing.

4. Choose **Save**, **Import flow**.

5. Select the file to import, and choose **Import**.

6. Review and update any resolved or unresolved references as necessary.

7. To save the imported flow, choose **Save**. To publish, choose **Save and Publish**.

Using Text-to-Speech with Amazon Connect

Amazon Connect supports text-to-speech, including SSML or plaintext with (or without) dynamic attributes. You can enter text-to-speech prompts in any of the contact flow blocks that support prompt entry, such as **Play prompt** and **Get customer input**. The text-to-speech voice is selected in the **Set voice** contact block. You can also use SSML in Amazon Lex bots to modify the voice used by a chat bot when interacting with your customers. For more information about using SSML in Amazon Lex bots, see Managing Messages and Managing Conversation Context in the Amazon Lex Developer Guide.

Amazon Connect uses Amazon Polly, a service that converts text into lifelike speech using Speech Synthesis Markup Language (SSML). For more information, see Using SSML in the Amazon Polly Developer Guide.

SSML-enhanced input text gives you more control over how Amazon Connect generates speech from the text you provide. You can customize and control aspects of speech such as pronunciation, volume, and speed. Amazon Polly provides this level of control using a subset of the SSML markup tags as defined by Speech Synthesis Markup Language (SSML) Version 1.1, W3C Recommendation.

Modify a Prompt using SSML

When you add a prompt to a contact flow, you can use SSML tags to provide a more personalized experience for your customers. The default setting in a contact flow block for interpreting text to speech is **Text**. To use SSML for text to speech in your contact flow blocks, set the **Interpret as** field to **SSML** as shown in the following image.

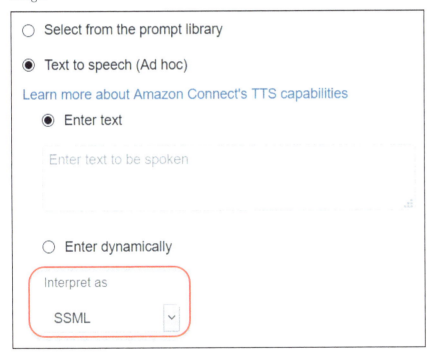

The following SSML tags are supported in Amazon Connect:

- speak
- break
- lang
- mark
- p
- phoneme
- prosody

- s
- say-as
- sub
- w
- amazon:effect name="whispered"

If you use an unsupported tag in your input text it is automatically ignored when it is processed. To learn more about the SSML tags, see SSML Tags in Amazon Polly.

Configuring Interactive Voice Response Workflows

You can ensure effective customer contact handling with interactive voice response (IVR) workflows, using queues, contact flows, and quick connects. These workflows provide a seamless customer experience, funneling contacts to the correct agents, and ensuring SLA adherence.

Claiming Phone Numbers

You can claim a phone number when you first create an instance, from the **Dashboard**, or you can claim one from the **Manage phone numbers** screen. You can also release a number that you no longer use.

Note
There is a limit of 10 numbers per contact center. If you reach your limit and no longer need a number, you can release it to make space for a new number. To do this, choose **Release**, **Release**. You cannot claim the same number again.

To claim a number for your contact center

1. Choose **Routing**, **Phone numbers**.

2. Choose **Claim a number** in the top-right corner of the screen. You can choose a **Toll free** or a **DID (Direct Inward Dialing)** number. **Note**
   If you want to select a number from a country, but there are no numbers displayed for that country when you select it, you can request additional numbers for that country using the Amazon Connect service limits increase form.
   If you want to keep a phone number you already have, you can port the phone number and use it with Amazon Connect. To learn more, see Port Your Current Phone Number.

3. Enter a description for the number and, if required, attach it to a contact flow in **Contact flow / IVR**.

4. Choose **Save**.

You can repeat this process until you have claimed all your required numbers.

You can add or edit descriptions, assign queues, and attach call flows to the numbers. You can also define an IVR workflow, which includes prompts, to support customer self-service.

To associate a phone number with a contact flow

1. Choose **Routing**, **Phone numbers**.

2. You can search for a specific number, filter your search by queue, or select a number from the list provided (if applicable).

3. Select the number to edit, expand **Contact flow / IVR**, and select the contact flow.

4. Choose **Save**.

Making International Calls

Amazon Connect uses the E.164 format for international dialing. This formatting is pre-configured in the CCP.

Creating Prompts

Prompts are audio files played in call flows. Only 8 KHz .wav files that are less than 50 MB are supported for prompts. You can upload a pre-recorded .wav file to use for your prompt, or record one in the web application. Prompts and routing policies should be aligned with each other to ensure a smooth call flow for customers.

To create a prompt

1. Choose **Routing**, **Prompts**.

2. On the **Manage voice prompts** screen, choose **+Create new prompt**.

3. You can choose the following actions:

   - **Upload**—Choose the file to upload.
   - **Record**—Choose the red circle to begin recording. Use the red square to stop. You can choose **Crop** to cut the recorded prompt or **Discard** to record a new prompt.

4. For **Step 2: Input basic information**, enter the name of the file, and then choose **Create**.

To manage recorded prompts

1. Choose **Routing**, **Prompts**.

2. On the **Manage voice prompts** screen, select the appropriate prompt.

3. You can choose **Play**, **Download**, **Edit**, or **Delete**.

4. Choose **Save**.

Creating Hours of Operation

Hours of operation define when a queue is available, and may be referenced in contact flows. Hours of operation are a required component when setting up queues, and must be completed first.

To add hours of operation in the console

1. Choose **Routing**, **Hours of operation**.

2. To create a template, choose **Add new hours** and enter a name and a description.

3. For **Time zone**, select a value.

4. For **Add new**, set new hours.

5. Choose **Save**.

Managing Queues

A queue is list of incoming contacts to be serviced by agents. You can use a single queue to handle all incoming contacts, or you can set up queues mapped to agents with specific skill sets.

Amazon Connect uses an automatic call distributor (ACD) to distribute incoming contacts to specific resources or agents within the call center, based on the selections made within the IVR. If an agent with a skill set matching the selection is not available the customer is placed in a pre-defined queue.

Calls in a queue are automatically prioritized and forwarded to the next available agent. Customers are placed on hold if there are no available agents. The order in which they are serviced is determined by their time in queue, on a first-come, first-served basis. If multiple resources are available, the call is routed to the agent who has had the **Available** status for the longest time.

Note
Routing profiles may create an exception where one queue takes priority over another, but the priority within the queue is always set by the order the contact was received. For more information, see Configuring Interactive Voice Response Workflows.

Accurate queue management and configuration ensures that an accurate spread of resources, and minimizes customer hold time. It also ensures that resources can be effectively rerouted during busy periods. You can have unlimited concurrent active queues.

Queue metrics can be monitored and reviewed using both real-time and historical metrics. Metrics include **Service Level**, **Average Handle Time**, **Average Abandon Time**, and **Average Hold Time**.

To create a new queue

1. Choose **Routing**, **Queues**, **Add new queue**.

2. Add the appropriate information about your queue and choose **Add new queue**.

Important
When you create a queue, you can specify an **Outbound caller ID name** and **Outbound caller ID number**. You can also provide a phone number in a **Set callback number** block in a contact flow. The callback name and number is sent as the origination party when Amazon Connect initiates the call to the destination. However, the information displayed to the person called may not always match the name or number set during call initiation. In some cases, the callback name is provided by the carrier of the person you are calling. The information may not be up-to-date with that carrier, or the number may get passed differently between systems due to hardware or configuration differences. If this is the case, the person that you call may not see the phone number, or may see the name of a previously registered owner of the number, instead of the name of the registered person from your organization.

When you create a queue, it is automatically active and can be assigned to a routing profile. Users with the proper permissions can deactivate the queue, which puts it in an offline mode and makes it unavailable to assign to a routing profile.

To disable an active queue

1. Choose **Routing**, **Queues**.

2. Hover over the name of the queue to edit and choose the power icon.

3. Choose **Disable**.

To reactivate a queue, follow the same steps as above.

To edit a queue

1. Choose **Routing**, **Queues**, and select the queue to edit.

2. Edit the queue details as required.

3. Choose **Save**.

Creating Quick Connects

Calls can be transferred to an agent, a queue, or an external number.

- **External**—Calls are transferred to an external number (such as an on-call pager).
- **Agent**—Calls are transferred to a specific agent as part of a contact flow.
- **Queue**—Calls are transferred to a queue as part of a contact flow.

To add a quick connect

1. Choose **Routing**, **Quick connects**, **Add a new destination**.

2. Enter a name for the item, and select a type, destination, contact flow (if applicable), and description.
   Important
   A description is required when you create a quick connect. An error is returned if you do not add a description.

3. To add more rows, choose **Add a new destination**.

4. Choose **Save**.

To see your quick connects in the contact list in CCP, add them to **Queues**. Agent and queue quick connects only appear when an agent transfers a call.

Working with Hierarchies

You can manage and load-balance customer contacts using agent hierarchy organization and agent status management. These tools provide filtering and agent availability management per queue, skill set, and routing profiles.

Hierarchies do not determine agent permissions or security settings. They define the organizational structure of agent groups for effective reporting.

Understanding Agent Hierarchy

Agents and teams can be organized into groupings based on their location and their skill sets. Hierarchies can be configured with up to five levels and allow you to segment agents or teams. You can create large groups, such as all agents who work on a specific continent, or smaller groups such as all agents working in a specific department. The hierarchies are reflected in reports and historical metrics to allow for granulated reporting. Removing agents from a level affects historical reporting until a new reporting cycle for that level has been completed.

Permissions can be set to restrict the visibility of data and ability to create hierarchies.

To configure a new agent hierarchy

1. Choose **Contact management**, **Agent hierarchy**.

2. Enter a name and choose + to create the first level of your hierarchy.

3. Choose + to add more levels to your hierarchy.

4. Choose **Save** to apply the changes, or **Cancel** to undo them.

When a hierarchy has been created, you can add groups, teams, and agents from the top down.

To add groupings to a hierarchy

1. Select the top level of the hierarchy.

2. Choose **x** to add groupings to each level.

3. Choose the check icon to save the name, choose the pencil icon to edit the name.

4. Choose **Save**.

Choose **View historical changes** to view the change history. You can filter changes by date (between two dates) or by user name. If you cannot see the link, ensure that you have the proper permissions to view these changes.

Managing Agent Status

Agent status is used for reporting and metrics, as well as resource management. Amazon Connect provides default editable states, but custom status values can be added. Customized agent status values are auxiliary by default.

To add a new agent status

1. Choose **Contact management**, **Agent status**, **Add new agent status**.

2. Enter a status name, description, and type, and select whether the status should be enabled in the CCP.

3. Choose **Save**.

To edit a status

1. Choose **Contact management**, **Agent status**.

2. Hover over the status name and choose the pencil icon.

3. Enter the new information, and choose **Save** to apply the changes.

Choose **View Historical Changes** to view the change history. You can filter changes by date (between two dates) or by user name. If you cannot see the **View historical changes** link, ensure that you have the proper permissions to view these changes.

Login/Logout Reports

The Login/Logout report displays the login and logout information for the agents in your Amazon Connect instance. For each agent session, the login and logout times are displayed as a row in the report. You can use the report to determine the time your agents were logged in to Amazon Connect. The report also displays the amount of time for each session that an agent was logged in to Amazon Connect.

Important
A Login/Logout report can contain up to 10,000 rows. When you generate a Login/Logout report that includes more than 10,000 rows, the report fails to complete. If you generate a report and view it on the Login/Logout report page, you receive an error if you attempt to display a page of the report beyond row 10,000. If you schedule a Login/Logout report that contains more than 10,000 rows, the report fails, no report output is saved to your S3 bucket, and you cannot view the report.
If you have a contact center with a lot of agents, and your reports fail to complete, you can specify a shorter time range to reduce the size of the report generated, or apply filters to the report, such as routing profile and agent hierarchy. You can then use other filters to capture all of the login / logout data for your instance. For more information, see Generate a Login/Logout Report.

You can view the report in the Amazon Connect interface, download the report, or share it with other users. You can set a schedule for the days of the week to generate the report, and you can filter the report on agent, agent hierarchy, or routing profile to include only records for a specific set of agents in the report.

Important
Only users that are assigned **Login/Logout report** permission see the **Login/Logout report** listed under **Metrics and quality**. Your Amazon Connect admin can grant or remove permissions. Closing the browser does not log the user out. The report does not show that a user has logged out until the user clicks the logout button. The user is shown as logged in from the previous login until the next time the user clicks the logout button.

Login/Logout Report Permissions

By default, only users assigned the Admin security profile for an Amazon Connect instance are granted permission to generate and view the Login/Logout reports. To allow other users to view a shared report, or to schedule or generate the report, your Amazon Connect admin must assign the Login/Logout report permission to a role assigned to that user. To enable other users in other roles to generate or view the reports, add the permission to the security role assigned to those users.

In Amazon Connect, permissions are assigned to security profiles. The permission a user has is determined by the security role assigned to the user account. Only users that are assigned a security profile that has been granted the View permission for Login/Logout reports can view published reports. If you share a link with a specific user, that user can only view the report if his or her account has explicit permission to do so via their security profile. If you do not want to grant the permission to one of the security profiles included with Amazon Connect, you can create a custom security profile and assign permissions to that role. Users can be assigned more than one security profile, so you could make a profile that grants permissions only to Login/Logout reports and then assign specified users to that profile.

To assign Login/Logout report permissions

1. Open the Amazon Connect dashboard.

2. Choose **Users, Security profiles**.

3. Select the security profile for which to modify permissions.

4. Choose **Metrics and Quality**.

5. In the **Login/Logout report** row, select **All** to grant all permissions, or **View** to only grant permissions to view shared reports.

6. Choose **Save**.

Generate a Login/Logout Report

When you generate a Login/Logout report, it includes only login or logout actions by your agents that occurred during the specified time range. If an agent logged in during the time range and did not log out, the report shows a login time but not a logout time. If the agent logged in before the start of the time range, and then logged out during the time range, the report shows both the login and logout times even though the login occurred before the start of the time range. This is so you can view the duration of the agent session associated with the most recent logout.

When you create your report, you can filter the results in the report by **Agent**, **Agent hierarchy**, **Routing profile**, or **None (show all agents)**. For the time frame, you can select **Today (since 12 am)**, **Last 24 hours**, **Yesterday**, **Last 2 days**, **Last 3 days**, or **Custom time range**.

To generate a Login/Logout report

1. Open your Amazon Connect dashboard.

2. Choose **Metrics and Quality**, **Login/Logout report**.

3. On the **Login/Logout report** page, choose the **Time range** for the records to include in the report.

4. Choose the **Time zone** to use for your report.

5. To filter data included in the report, for **Filter by**, choose a value.

6. Choose **Generate report**, **Save**.

7. Provide a name for the report, and choose **Save**.

Edit a Saved Login/Logout Report

After you save your report, you can edit it at any time. When you open a saved report, the time frame and date range displayed show the date and time defined when you saved the report.

To edit a saved Login/Logout report

1. Open your Amazon Connect dashboard.

2. Choose **Metrics and quality**, **Saved reports**.

3. Choose **Login/Logout report** and select the report to edit.

4. Update the **Time range**, **Time zone**, and **Filter by** settings.

5. To overwrite your existing report, choose **Save**.

6. To save the changes as a new report, choose **Save**, **Save as**. Provide a name for the report and choose **Save as**.

Download a Login/Logout Report as a CSV File

When you have generated a report, you can download it as a comma-separated value (CSV) file so that you can use it other applications to work with the data, such as a spreadsheet or database.

To download a report as a CSV file

1. Open the report to download.

2. On the **Login/Logout report** page, at the top right corner, choose the **Share report** menu (arrow) next to **Save**.

3. Choose **Download CSV**. The file Login_Logout report.csv is downloaded to your computer.

Share a Login/Logout Report

To make the report available to other people in your organization, you can share a report. People can access the report only if they have appropriate permissions in Amazon Connect.

To share a Login/Logout report

1. On the **Login/Logout report** page, at the top right corner, choose the **Share report** menu (arrow) next to **Save**.

2. Choose **Share report**.

3. To copy the URL to the report, choose **Copy link address**. You can send the URL to others in your organization by pasting the link into an email or other document.

4. To publish the report to your organization, for **Publish report to organization**, move the toggle to **On**.

5. Choose **Save**.

Schedule a Login/Logout Report

To generate a report with the same settings on a regular basis, you can schedule the report to run daily or on specific days of the week. When you schedule a report, it is automatically published to your organization. Anyone with appropriate permissions can view the report. Users with all permissions for Login/Logout reports can also edit, schedule, or delete the report.

When you schedule your report, keep in mind that the report always runs at 12AM on the day you select, in the time zone that you choose. If you select Wednesday, the report runs at midnight Wednesday and does not include any data for Wednesday. Scheduled reports are saved as CSV files in your Amazon S3 bucket. The default time zone is UTC. To have your report run at 12AM in your local time, choose your time zone instead.

To schedule a Login/Logout report

1. If you already have a saved report to schedule open, skip to step 4. Otherwise, in the dashboard, choose **Metrics and quality**, **Saved reports**.

2. Choose **Login/Logout report**.

3. Hover the mouse pointer over the row containing the name of the report to schedule, and choose the **Schedule report** icon.

4. On the **Schedule report** page, under **Recurrence**, for **Generate this report**, choose whether to generate the report **Daily** or **Weekly**.

5. If you choose **Weekly**, select the day or days of the week on which to run the report.

6. Choose the **Time zone**.

7. To add a prefix to the S3 path to the saved report, choose **Delivery Options** and enter a value in the **Prefix** field.

   The prefix is added to the path between /Reports and the report name. For example: .../Reports/*my-prefix*/report-name-YYYY-MM-DD...

8. Choose **Create**.

After you schedule a report, you can change or delete the schedule for it at any time.

To edit or delete the schedule for a report

1. Follow the steps in the preceding section to open the **Schedule report** page.

2. To edit the schedule, choose **Edit**, update the **Recurrence** and **Delivery Options** as desired, and then choose **Save**.

3. To delete the schedule for the report, choose **Delete**, and then choose **Delete** again on the confirmation dialog.

Delete a Saved Login/Logout Report

Too many reports in your report library? If you no longer want to use a saved report, you can delete it. When you delete a report, you are only deleting the settings for the report, not any reports that have already been generated using those settings. No CSV files created from a scheduled report are removed from your S3 bucket.

To delete a saved Login/Logout report

1. Open your Amazon Connect dashboard.

2. Choose **Metrics and quality, Saved reports**.

3. Hover over the row for the report to delete, and choose the **Delete** icon.

4. Choose **Delete** again.

Agent Event Streams

Amazon Connect agent event streams are Amazon Kinesis data streams that provide you with near real-time reporting of agent activity within your Amazon Connect instance. The events published to the stream include agent login, agent logout, agent answers a call, and agent status change.

You can use the agent event streams to create dashboards that display agent information and events, integrate streams into workforce management (WFM) solutions, and configure alerting tools to trigger custom notifications of specific agent activity. Agent event streams help you manage agent staffing and efficiency.

Enabling Agent Event Streams

Agent event streams are not enabled by default. Before you can enable agent event streams in Amazon Connect, create a data stream in Amazon Kinesis Data Streams. Then, choose the Kinesis stream as the stream to use for agent event streams. Though you can use the same stream for both agent event streams and contact trace records, managing and getting data from the stream is much easier when you use a separate stream for each. For more information, see the Amazon Kinesis Data Streams Developer Guide.

Note
If you enable server-side encryption for the Kinesis stream you select for agent event streams, Amazon Connect cannot publish to the stream because it does not have permission to kms:GenerateDataKey. No records are published to the stream.

To enable agent event streams

1. Open the Amazon Connect console at https://console.aws.amazon.com/connect/.

2. On the console, choose the name in the **Instance Alias** column of the instance for which to enable agent event streams.

3. Choose **Data streaming**, then select **Enable data streaming**.

4. Under **Agent Events**, select the Kinesis stream to use, and then choose **Save**.

Agent Event Streams Data Model

Agent event streams are created in JavaScript Object Notation (JSON) format. For each event type, a JSON blob is sent to the Kinesis data stream. The following event types are included in agent event streams:

- LOGIN—An agent login to the contact center.
- LOGOUT—An agent logout from the contact center.
- STATE_CHANGE—One of the following changed:
  - Agent configuration, such as profile or the assigned hierarchy group.
  - Agent state in the contact control panel, such as Available.
  - Agent conversation state, such as on hold.
- HEART_BEAT—This event is published every 120 seconds if there are no other events published during that interval.

Each agent event type blob includes the following data about the event.

AgentEvent

The `AgentEvent` object includes the following properties:

AgentARN
The Amazon Resource Name (ARN) for the agent. To find the ARN for an agent, open the user settings for the

user in Amazon Connect. The ARN is displayed in the address bar.
Type: ARN

AWSAccountId
The 12-digit AWS account ID for the AWS account associated with the Amazon Connect instance.
Type: String

CurrentAgentSnapshot
Contains agent configuration, such as username, first name, last name, routing profile, hierarchy groups, contacts, and agent status.
Type: `AgentSnapshot` object

EventId
Universally unique identifier (UUID) for the event.
Type: String

EventTimestamp
A time stamp for the event, in ISO 8601 standard format.
Type: String (*yyyy-mm-dd*T*hh:mm:ss*Z)

EventType
The type of event.
Valid values: `STATE_CHANGE` | `HEART_BEAT` | `LOGIN` | `LOGOUT`

InstanceARN
Amazon Resource Name for the Amazon Connect instance in which the agent's user account is created.
Type: ARN

PreviousAgentSnapshot
Contains agent configuration, such as username, first name, last name, routing profile, hierarchy groups), contacts, and agent status. Not applicable to LOGIN or LOGOUT events.
Type: `AgentSnapshot` object

Version
The version of the agent event stream in date format, such as 2017-10-10.
Type: String

AgentSnapshot

The `AgentSnapshot` object includes the following properties:

AgentStatus
Agent status data, including:

- AgentARN—the ARN for the agent.
- Name—the name of the status, such as Available or Offline. Type: `AgentStatus` object.

Configuration
Information about the agent, including:

- FirstName—the agent's first name.
- HierarchyGroups—the hierarchy group the agent is assigned to, if any.
- LastName—the agent's last name.
- RoutingProfile—the routing profile the agent is assigned to.
- Username—the agent's Amazon Connect user name. Type: `Configuration` object

Contacts
List of contacts
Type: `ContactList` object

Configuration

The `Configuration` object includes the following properties:

FirstName
The first name entered in the agent's Amazon Connect account.
Type: String
Length: 1-100

AgentHierarchyGroups
The hierarchy group, up to five levels of grouping, for the agent associated with the event.
Type: `AgentHierarchyGroups` object

LastName
The last name entered in the agent's Amazon Connect account.
Type: String
Length: 1-100

RoutingProfile
The routing profile assigned to the agent associated with the event.
Type: `RoutingProfile` object.

Username
The user name for the agent's Amazon Connect user account.
Type: String
Length: 1-100

Contact Object

The `Contact` object includes the following properties:

ContactId
UUID identifier for the contact
Type: String
Length: 1-256

InitialContactId
The `ContactId` of the original contact that was transferred.
Type: String
Length: 1-256

Channel
Enumeration of the method of communication, such as Voice.
Valid values: `VOICE`

InitiationMethod
How the contact was initiated.
Valid values: `INBOUND` | `OUTBOUND` | `TRANSFER` | `CALLBACK` | `API`

State
An enumeration of the state of the contact.
Valid values: `INCOMING` | `PENDING` | `CONNECTING` | `CONNECTED` | `CONNECTED_ONHOLD` | `MISSED` | `ERROR` | `ENDED`

StateStartTimestamp
A time stamp for the time at which the contact entered the State.
Type: String (*yyyy-mm-dd*T*hh:mm:ss*Z)

ConnectedToAgentTimestamp
A time stamp for the time the contact was connected to an agent.
Type: String (*yyyy-mm-dd*T*hh:mm:ss*Z)

QueueTimestamp
A time stamp for the time at which the contact was put into a queue.
Type: String (*yyyy-mm-dd*T*hh:mm:ss*Z)

Queue
The queue the contact was placed in.
Type: `Queue` object

HierarchyGroup Object

The `HierarchyGroup` object includes the following properties:

ARN
The Amazon Resource Name for the agent hierarchy.
Type: String

Name
The name of the hierarchy group.
Type: String

AgentHierarchyGroups Object

The `AgentHierarchyGroups` object includes the following properties:

Level1
Includes details for Level1 of the hierarchy assigned to the agent.
Type: `HierarchyGroup` object

Level2
Includes details for Level2 of the hierarchy assigned to the agent.
Type: `HierarchyGroup` object

Level3
Includes details for Level3 of the hierarchy assigned to the agent.
Type: `HierarchyGroup` ob4ject

Level4
Includes details for Level4 of the hierarchy assigned to the agent.
Type: `HierarchyGroup` object

Level5
Includes details for Level5 of the hierarchy assigned to the agent.
Type: `HierarchyGroup` object

Queue Object

The `Queue` object includes the following properties:

ARN
Amazon Resource Name for the queue.
Type: String

Name
The name of the queue.
Type: String

RoutingProfile Object

The `RoutingProfile` object includes the following properties:

ARN
Amazon Resource Name for the agent's routing profile.
Type: String

Name
The name of the routing profile.
Type: String

InboundQueues
A list of `Queue` objects associated with the agent's routing profile.
Type: List of `Queue` object

DefaultOutboundQueue
The default outbound queue for the agent's routing profile.
Type: `Queue` object

Amazon Connect Contact Attributes

Topics

- Using Contact Attributes
- User-Defined Attributes
- System Attributes for Contact Flows
- External Attributes
- Using Contact Attributes to Personalize the Customer Experience
- Use Amazon Connect Contact Attributes with Other Services
- Using Attributes in the Contact Control Panel
- Referencing Contact Attributes
- Using System Metric Attributes
- Contact Attributes Available in Amazon Connect
- System Metrics Attributes

In Amazon Connect, a contact is an interaction with a customer in your contact center. The interaction can be a voice phone call with a human agent, or an automated interaction using an Amazon Lex bot. Contact attributes in Amazon Connect refer to key-value pairs of data about a contact.

Using contact attributes, you can customize and personalize the experience customers have when they interact with your contact center. Contact attributes let you store customer input or data about a customer, and then use it later in a contact flow. You can also check the values of contact attributes and use a condition to determine the branching behavior of the contact flow based on the value.

Contact attributes let you pass data between Amazon Connect and other services, such as Amazon Lex and AWS Lambda. Contact attributes can be both set and consumed by each service. For example, you could use a Lambda function to look up customer information, such as their name or order number, and use contact attributes to store the values returned to Amazon Connect. You could then reference those attributes to include the customer's name in messages using text to speech, or store their order number so they do not have to enter it again.

Using Contact Attributes

When you create a contact flow, you can create user-defined contact attributes using **Set contact attributes** blocks. You can then reference them in other parts of a contact flow using any other block that supports dynamic attributes. For example, you could use a **Check contact attributes** block to compare the value of an attribute to a condition you define, and then route the contact based on the comparison. You could also retrieve data from external sources, and then create user-defined attributes from the external data so that you can reference them later in a contact flow, such as the status of an order or an expected shipping date.

Personalize the customer experience by including the customer's name when you use text to speech text in a **Play prompt** or **Get customer input** block to speak messages to your customer. Use contact attributes to store input provided by a customer during an interaction with a Amazon Lex bot to enable automated interactions.

As a best practice, treat attributes and attribute values as case-sensitive, and always match case in each context where they are used.

There are three types of contact attributes in Amazon Connect:

- *User-defined*—These attributes are created during the execution of a contact flow using **Set contact attributes** blocks. When you get data from an external source, you can copy key-value pairs as user-defined attributes to reference later in a contact flow. User-defined attributes can also be created through the Amazon Connect API.
- *System*—These are predefined attributes in Amazon Connect. You can reference system attributes, but you cannot create them. There are system attributes related to contacts, and system attributes related to metrics.

- *External*—These attributes are created via a process external to Amazon Connect, such as when you use an **Invoke AWS Lambda function** block in a contact flow, or integrate with an Amazon Lex bot.

User-Defined Attributes

User-defined attributes include all attributes set by using a **Set contact attributes** block in a contact flow. User-defined attributes are included in contact trace records (CTRs), are available to Lambda functions that are invoked after the **Set contact attributes** block, and are created in the Attributes namespace. They are also available to applications that integrate with the CCP for screenpop information, and can be referenced in contact flows.

System Attributes for Contact Flows

There are four system attributes related to contacts available in contact flow blocks.

- **Customer number**—The phone number of the customer. The phone number of the customer. This attribute is included in the CTRs and Lambda input object under CustomerEndpoint.
- **Dialed number**—The number that the customer dialed to reach your contact center. This attribute is included in the CTRs and Lambda input under SystemEndpoint.
- **Customer callback number**—The number that the system uses to call the customer back, either for the **Transfer to callback** queue functionality, or for an agent dialing from the CCP. The default value is the number the customer used to call your contact center, but can be overwritten with the **Set callback number** block. This attribute is not included in CTRs, and not accessible in Lambda input. You can copy the attribute to a user-defined attribute with the **Set contact attribute** block, which is included in CTRs. You can also pass this attribute as a Lambda input parameter in an **Invoke AWS Lambda function** block, which is not included in CTRs.
- **Stored customer input**—The attribute values created from the most recent **Store customer input** block invocation. This attribute is not included in CTRs, and is not accessible in Lambda input. You can copy the attribute to a user-defined attribute with the **Set contact attribute** block, which is included in CTRs. You can also pass this attribute as a Lambda input parameter in an **Invoke AWS Lambda function** block, which is not included in CTRs. This attribute value applies only to the most recent invocation of the Lambda function. It is overwritten with the next invocation of the function.

External Attributes

External attributes are returned as key-value pairs from the most recent invocation of an **Invoke AWS Lambda function** block. External attributes are overwritten with each invocation of the Lambda function. You can access external attributes in contact flows via $.External.AttributeName. For more information about using attributes in Lambda functions, see Granting Amazon Connect Access to AWS Lambda Functions.

These attributes are not included in CTRs, not passed to the next Lambda invocation, and not passed to the CCP for screenpop information. However, they can be passed as Lambda function inputs on an **Invoke AWS Lambda function** block, or copied to user-defined attributes via the **Set contact attributes** block. When used in **Set contact attributes** blocks, the attributes that are copied are included in CTRs, and can be used in the CCP.

Using Contact Attributes to Personalize the Customer Experience

Contact attributes in your contact flows can provide a more personalized customer experience. For example, specify a custom call flow based on comparing an attribute to a value, and then route the call based on the value comparison, such as routing customers to different tiers of support based on their account number. Or retrieve a customer's name, save the name as an attribute, and then include the name attribute in a text to speech string so that the customer's name is said during the interaction.

The steps in the following sections describe how to use contact attributes with different blocks in a contact flow.

Using a Set Contact Attributes Block

Use a **Set contact attributes** block to set a value that is later referenced in a contact flow. For example, you could create a personalized greeting for customers routed to a queue based on the type of customer account, or define an attribute for a company name or line of business to include in text to speech strings said to a customer. The **Set contact attributes** block is useful for copying attributes retrieved from external sources to user-defined attributes.

To set a contact attribute with a Set contact attributes block

1. In Amazon Connect, choose **Routing, Contact flows**.

2. Select an existing contact flow, or create a new one.

3. Add a **Set contact attributes** block.

4. Edit the **Set contact attributes** block, and choose **Save text as attribute**.

5. For the **Destination** key, provide a name for the attribute, such as *Company*. For the **Value**, use your company name.

Capture Customer Input and Store it as an Attribute

You can use an attribute to request a callback number from a customer, store the value of the attribute, and then reference the attribute in a **Set callback number** block to set the number to dial the customer. You could also use a **Store customer input** block to capture any numeric input from a customer, such as an account or order number.

To create an attribute from customer input with a Store customer input block

1. In Amazon Connect, choose **Routing, Contact flows**.

2. Select an existing contact flow, or create a new one.

3. Add a **Store customer input** block.

4. Edit the block, and select **Text to speech (Ad hoc)**.

5. In the **Enter text** box, type a message that is said to customers when they call, such as "Please enter your phone number."

6. In the **Customer input** section, select **Phone number**, and then choose the format. **Local format** is for a number in the same country as the region in which you created your Amazon Connect instance. **International format/Enforce E.164** is for numbers to a country other than the country in which you created your instance.

Store customer input

Stores numerical input to contact attribute.

Prompt

○ Select from the prompt library

◉ Text to speech (Ad hoc)

Learn more about Amazon Connect's TTS capabilities

◉ Enter text

> Please enter your phone number.

○ Enter dynamically

Interpret as

Text ⌄

Prompt

○ Custom

◉ Phone number

◉ Local format

Country code   Delay between entry

🇺🇸 +1 ▼   5

in seconds

7. Add a **Set callback number** block to your contact flow, and connect it to the **Get customer input** block.

8. Under **Use attributes**, for **Type**, choose **System**. For **Attribute**, choose **Stored customer input**. The callback number is set to the number the customer entered when asked to enter their phone number.

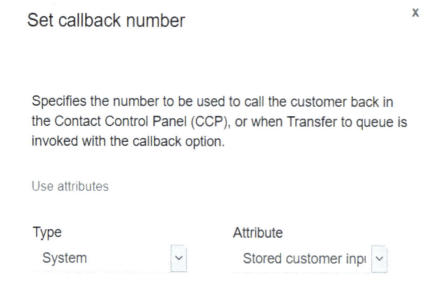

Using Attributes with a Lambda Function

Retrieve data from a system your organization uses internally, such as an ordering system or other database with a Lambda function, and store the values as attributes that can then be referenced in a contact flow.

When the Lambda function returns a response from your internal system, the response is key-value pairs of data. You can reference the values returned in the External namespace, for example $.External.attributeName. To use the attributes later in a contact flow, you can copy the key-value pairs to user-defined attributes using a **Set contact attributes** block. You can then define logic to branch your contact based on attribute values by using a **Check contact attributes** block. Any contact attribute retrieved from a Lambda function is overwritten with the next invocation of a Lambda function. Make sure you store external attributes if you want to reference them later in a contact flow.

To store an external value from a Lambda function as a contact attribute

1. In Amazon Connect, choose **Routing, Contact flows**.

2. Select an existing contact flow, or create a new one.

3. Add an **Invoke AWS Lambda function** block.

4. Add the **Function ARN** to your AWS Lambda function that retrieves customer data from your internal system.

5. After the **Invoke AWS Lambda function** block, add a **Set contact attributes** block and connect the **Success** branch of the **Invoke AWS Lambda function** block to it.

6. Edit the **Set contact attributes** block, and select **Use attribute**.

7. For the **Type**, choose **External**.

8. For **Destination key**, type a name to use as a reference to the attribute, such as customerName.

9. For **Source attribute** type the name of the attribute returned from the Lambda function. The name of the attribute returned from the function will vary depending on your internal system and the funtion you

use.

Set contact attributes ✕

Stores key / value pairs as contact attributes.

Contact attributes are accessible by other areas of Amazon
Connect, such as the Contact Control Panel (CCP) and Contact
Trace Records (CTRs).

Attribute to save

○ Save text as attribute ✕

◉ Use attribute

Type

External ⌄

Destination key   Source attribute

customerName $.External.customerName

Add another attribute

After this block executes during a contact flow, the value is saved as a user-defined attribute with the name specified by the **Destination key**, in this case customerName. It can be accessed in any block that uses dynamic attributes.

To branch your contact flow based on the value of an external attribute, such as an account number, use a **Check contact attributes** block, and then add a condition to compare the value of the attribute to. Next, branch the contact flow route based on the condition.

---

1. In the **Check contact attributes** block, for **Attribute to check** do one of the following:
   - Select **External** and then type the key name returned from the Lambda function. **Important** Any attribute returned from an AWS Lambda function is overwritten with the next function invocation. To reference them later in a contact flow, store them as user-defined attributes.
   - Select **User defined** and then type the name that you specified as the **Destination key** in the **Set contact attributes** block.
2. Choose **Add another condition**.
3. Under **Conditions to check**, choose the comparison type and specify a value to compare to. A branch is created for each comparison you enter, letting you route the contact based on the conditions specified. If no condition is matched, the contact takes the **No Match** branch from the block.

Use Amazon Connect Contact Attributes with Other Services

You can reference contact attributes set in your Amazon Connect contact flow in other services, such as in an Amazon Lex bot or AWS Lambda function, so that data associated with the customer or the contact can be shared between services for a seamless customer experience. To use contact attributes to access other resources, set a user-defined attribute in your contact flow and use the Amazon Resource Name (ARN) of the resource you want to access as the value for the attribute. For example, to use an Amazon Connect prompt in a Lambda function, set a user-defined attribute to the ARN for the prompt, and then access that attribute from the Lambda function.

Using Attributes in the Contact Control Panel

Contact attributes also let you capture information and then present that information in a screenpop to an agent in the Contact Control Panel (CCP). Use contact attributes to customize the agent experience when using the CCP integrated with a customer relationship management (CRM) application. Also use them when integrating Amazon Connect with a custom application using the Amazon Connect Streams API or Amazon Connect API. You can use all user-defined attributes, in addition to the customer number and the dialed number, in the CCP using the Amazon Connect Streams JavaScript library. For more information, see Amazon Connect Streams API or Amazon Connect API.

When you use the Amazon Connect Streams API, you can access user-defined attributes by invoking contact.getAttributes(). You can access endpoints via contact.getConnections(), where a connection has a getEndpoint() invocation on it.

To access the attribute directly from a Lambda function, use $.External.AttributeName. If the attribute is stored to a user-defined attribute from a **Set contact attributes** block, use $.Attributes.AttributeName.

For example, included with your Amazon Connect instance, there is a contact flow named "Sample note for screenpop." In this contact flow, a **Set contact attributes** block is used to create an attribute from a text string. The text, as an attribute, can be passed to the CCP to display a note to an agent.

Referencing Contact Attributes

The way you reference contact attributes depends on how they were created and how you are accessing them. To reference attributes in the same namespace, such as a system attribute, you use the attribute name, or the name you specified as the **Destination key**. To reference values in a different namespace, such as referencing an external attribute, you specify the JSONPath syntax to the attribute.

For example, to reference a customer name from a Lambda function lookup, you would use $.External.AttributeName, replacing AttributeName with the name of the attribute returned from the Lambda function. To reference an attribute from an Amazon Lex bot, you use the format $.Lex. and then include the part of the Amazon Lex bot to reference, such as $.Lex.intentName or $.Lex.dialogState. To reference the customer input to an Amazon Lex bot slot, use $.Lex.Slots.slotName.

JSONPath is a standardized way to query elements of a JSON object. JSONPath uses path expressions to navigate elements, nested elements, and arrays in a JSON document. For more information about JSON, see Introducing JSON.

Referencing Attributes from a Check Contact Attributes Block

In the **Check contact attributes** block, set the **Attribute to check** to one of the following:

- **User Defined**—If you choose **User Defined**, in the second field, type the name of the attribute to compare to the condition. In the following image, the attribute to check is an intent from an Amazon Lex bot, and the conditions to check are input values to the bot to determine the user's intent.

- **External**—If you choose **External**, in the second field type the name of the attribute to compare to the condition. Define the conditions to check, and then when you save the block, a branch is added for each condition you specify. Determine how the contact is routed by connecting the branches to other blocks in your contact flow.
- **System**—If you choose **System**, specify the system attribute to compare to the condition.

Referencing Attributes from a Play Prompt Block

To use the values of a contact attribute to personalize a message for a customer, use a **Play prompt** block, and then include references to the stored contact attributes in the text-to-speech message. For example, if you retrieved the customer's name from a Lambda function, and it returns values from your customer database for FirstName and LastName, you could use these attributes to say the customer's name in the text-to-speech block by including text similar to the following:

Hello $.External.FirstName $.External.LastName, thank you for calling.

Alternatively, you could store the attributes returned from the Lambda function using a **Set contact attributes** block, and then reference the user-defined attribute created in the text to speech string.

Play prompt

X

Plays audio.

Prompts can be an audio file, stored in the prompt library, or text-to-speech, which can optionally be specified in a flow via a contact attribute.

Prompt

○ Select from the prompt library

◉ Text to speech (Ad hoc)

Learn more about Amazon Connect's TTS capabilities

◉ Enter text

> Hello $.External.FirstName $.External.LastName, thank you for calling.

○ Enter dynamically

Interpret as

Text ⌄

Getting Customer Input Using an Amazon Lex Bot

When you reference attributes in a **Get customer input** block, and choose Amazon Lex as the method of collecting the input, the attribute values are retrieved and stored from the output from the customer interaction with the Amazon Lex bot. You can use an attribute for each intent, dialog state, or slot used in the Amazon Lex bot. To reference these attributes in a contact flow, use the following format:

$.Lex.LexAttributeName, such as $.Lex.DialogState or $.Lex.IntentName

You can reference the value of a specific slot in the Amazon Lex bot by using the following format:

$.Lex.Slots.slotName where slotName is the name of the slot to reference in the Amazon Lex bot.

Get customer input

Configure the branches that a customer can choose based on their intent.

DTMF   **Amazon Lex**

Configure the branches that a customer can choose based on their intent.

Lex bot

Name	Alias
LexBotName	BotAlias

Session attributes

⦿ Send text

Key	Value
input1	customerInput1

✕

○ Send attribute

Add another parameter

Intents

✕   firstIntent

✕   secondIntent

Add another parameter

Using System Metric Attributes

Amazon Connect includes system metric attributes that can help you define routing conditions in your contact flows based on real-time metrics about the queues and agents in your contact center. When you include a **Get metrics** block in your contact flow, metrics are retrieved for the current working queue, or other queue that you specify, and returned as attributes in the Metrics namespace.

You can reference the metric attributes returned to determine the optimal route for a contact by checking current queue metrics, such as the number of contacts currently in a queue, the number of available agents in a queue, and the length of time the oldest contact has been in a queue. You could even get metrics for multiple queues and use a **Set contact attributes** block to store the metric attributes for each queue. You could then compare queue metric attributes using a **Check contact attributes** block, and route the contact to the queue with the fewest calls in it, or to a callback if all queues are busy. To learn more about the metric attributes available, see System Metrics Attributes.

To use system metrics attributes in a contact flow

1. In Amazon Connect, choose **Routing**, **Contact flows**.

2. Select an existing contact flow, or create a new one.

3. Add a **Get metrics** block to the contact flow.

4. Optionally, to specify a queue select the **Set queue** check box and do one of the following:

   - Select the queue to retrieve metrics for from the drop-down list.
   - Select **Use attribute**, and the select the attribute to use.

   If you do not select a queue, metrics are retrieved for the current working queue.

5. Copy the metric attributes to user-defined attributes by adding a **Set contact attributes** block to the contact flow. Connect the **Success** branch of the **Get metrics** block to it.

6. Edit the **Set contact attributes** block, and select **Save text as attribute**. For the **Destination key**, type a name for to use for the attribute, such as queueCount for the number of contacts currently in the queue. For **Value**, type the reference to the metric attribute in the metric namespace, such as $.Metrics.Queue.Count.

   This creates a user-defined attribute named queueCount that stores the value for the queue count metric.

7. Add a **Check contact attributes** block and connect the **Success** branch of the **Get metrics** block to it.

8. To create a branching condition based on the value of the metric, now a user-defined attribute, add a **Check contact attributes** block to the contact flow. Connect the Success branch of the Set contact attributes block to the Check contact attributes block.

9. Edit the **Check contact attributes** block. Under **Attribute to check**, choose **User Defined**. In the second field, type the reference to the metric attribute to copy, such as $.Metrics.Queue.Size.

10. For the **Conditions to check**, choose the conditions to compare the attribute value to, and then type a value in the **Value** field.

11. Add additional blocks to the contact flow, connecting the branch of the Check contact attributes block to route the call to the next block in the flow.

Be sure to save and publish the contact flow to make it available in your contact center.

Contact Attributes Available in Amazon Connect

The following sections describes the contact attributes available in Amazon Connect.

Contact Flow System Attributes

Attribute	Description	Type
Customer number	The customer's phone number.	System
Dialed number	The number the customer dialed to call your contact center.	System
Customer callback number	The number to dial to call back the customer.	System
Stored customer input	An attribute created from the most recent invocation of a **Store customer input ** block.	System

External Contact Attributes

The following table describes the external attributes from a Lambda function.

Attribute	Description	Type
ContactId	The unique identifier for the contact.	External
OriginalContactId	The unique identifier for the contact created for the first interaction the customer had with your contact center. Use the OriginalContactId to trace contacts between contact flows.	External
PreviousContactId	The unique identifier for the contact before it was transferred. You can use the PreviousContactId to trace contacts between contact flows.	External
Channel	The method of contact. Currently, only VOICE is supported in Amazon Connect.	External
InstanceARN	The ARN for your Amazon Connect instance.	External
InitiationMethod	How the contact was initiated. Valid values include: INBOUND, OUTBOUND, TRANSFER, CALLBACK, or API.	External
SystemEndpoint.Address	The number the customer dialed to reach your contact center.	External
CustomerEndpoint.Address	The customer's phone number.	External
Queue.Name	The name of the queue to route the contact to.	External
Queue.ARN	The ARN for the queue.	External

Attribute	Description	Type
TextToSpeechVoiceId	The name of the voice to use, such as Joanna, for text-to-speech phrases in a contact flow.	External

Contact Attributes from Amazon Lex

The following table lists the attributes available from Amazon Lex bots.

Attribute	Description	Type
dialogState	The last dialog state returned from an Amazon Lex bot. The value is 'Fulfilled' if an Intent was returned to the contact flow.	External
intentName	The user intent returned by Amazon Lex.	External
Slots	Map of intent slots (key/value pairs) Amazon Lex detected from the user input during the interaction.	External
sessionAttribute	Map of key-value pairs representing the session-specific context information.	External

System Metrics Attributes

The metrics attributes in the following table are returned when you use the **Get metrics** block to retrieve metrics for a queue. If there is no current activity in your contact center, null values are returned for these attributes.

Attribute	Description	Type
Queue.Name	The name of the queue.	System
Queue.ARN	The ARN for the queue.	System
TextToSpeechVoiceId	The name of the voice to use for text-to-speech.	System
ContactId	The unique identifier of the contact.	System
InitialContactId	The unique identifier for the first contact a customer had with your contact center. Use the InitialContactId to track contacts between contact flows.	System
PreviousContactId	The unique identifier for the contact before it was transferred. Use the PreviousContactId to trace contacts between contact flows.	System

Attribute	Description	Type
Channel	The method of contact. Currently, only VOICE is supported in Amazon Connect.	System
InstanceARN	The ARN for your Amazon Connect instance.	System
InitiationMethod	How the contact was initiated. Valid values include: INBOUND, OUTBOUND, TRANSFER, or CALLBACK.	System
SystemEndpoint.Type	The type of endpoint for a contact. Currently only TELEPHONE_NUMBER is supported.	System
SystemEndpoint.Address	The value for the system endpoint. Currently only a telephone number is supported.	System
CustomerEndpoint.Type	The type of endpoint for the customer. Currently only TELEPHONE_NUMBER is supported.	System
CustomerEndpoint.Address	The value for the customer endpoint. Currently only a telephone number is supported.	System
Queue.OutboundCallerId	The outbound caller ID number defined for the queue. This can be useful for reverting the caller ID after setting a custom caller ID.	System
Agent.UserName	The user name an agent uses to log in to Amazon Connect.	System
Agent.FirstName	The agent's first name as entered in their Amazon Connect user account.	System
Agent.LastName	The agent's last name as entered in their Amazon Connect user account.	System
Agent.ARN	The ARN of the agent.	System
Metrics.Queue.Name	The name of the queue for which metrics were retrieved.	System
Metrics.Queue.ARN	The ARN of the queue for which metrics were retrieved.	System
Metrics.Queue.Size	The number of contacts currently in the queue.	System
Metrics.Queue.OldestContactAge	For the contact that has been in the queue the longest, the length of time that the contact has been in the queue, in seconds.	System
Metrics.Agents.Online.Count	Number of agents currently online (in any state other than offline).	System

Attribute	Description	Type
Metrics.Agents.Available.Count	Number of agents whose state is set to Available.	System
Metrics.Agents.Staffed.Count	Number of agents currently staffed, which is agents in Available, ACW, or Busy states.	System
Metrics.Agents.AfterContactWork.Count	Number of agents currently in ACW state.	System
Metrics.Agents.Busy.Count	Number of agents currently active on a contact.	System
Metrics.Agents.Missed.Count	Number of agents in Missed state, which is the state an agent enters after a missed call.	System
Metrics.Agents.NonProductive.Count	Number of agents in a non-productive state.	System

Amazon Connect Metrics and Reports

In Amazon Connect, data about contacts, such as the amount of time a contact spends in each state (customer on hold, customer in queue, agent interaction time) are captured in contact trace records (CTR). The basis for most historical and real-time metrics in Amazon Connect is the data in the CTR. When you create metrics reports, the values displayed for most metrics in the report are calculated using the data captured in the CTRs.

Note
Not all metrics are derived from CTR data. For example, the **Contacts consulted** metric, which is a count of number of times an agent consulted with a third party, is not included in CTRs.

Within Amazon Connect, you can generate a number of real-time and historical metric reports to monitor efficiency and utilization, agent performance, and other information about your contact center. CTRs are available within your instance for 24 months. You can also choose to stream CTRs to Amazon Kinesis so that you can manage retention and perform advanced analysis on the data for your contact center.

To get detailed information on the activity of agents in your contact center, you can use Agent Event Streams.

Permissions Required to Access Metrics Reports

Only users with appropriate permissions can create and view metrics reports. The **QualityAnalyst** and **CallCenterManager** security profiles include the permissions necessary to access metric data, which allows for viewing metrics reports. To view metrics reports, a user account must be assigned the **Access** permission for **Access Metrics** under **Metrics and Quality** on the **Security profiles** page.

Real-time Metrics Reports

Real-time metrics reports show real-time or near-real time metrics information about activity in your contact center. Metrics such as **Online** show the number of agents currently online in real-time, updating every 15 seconds. Metrics such as **Handled** and **Abandoned** reflect near real-time values for your contact center. Data in Real-time reports is refreshed as follows:

- The report page updates every 15 seconds.
- Metrics such as **Active** and **Availability** update as activity occurs, with very a very small system delay for processing the activity.
- Agent near real-time metrics, such as **Missed** and **Occupancy**, update every 5 minutes.
- Contact near real-time metrics update about 1 minute after a contact ends.

Report templates are included for **Queues**, **Agents**, and **Routing profiles**. You can also customize each of the report types and specify a time range for the report and select filters for fields to include or exclude from the report. You can add additional reports, or display multiple versions of the same report type, and customize each to include different information or a different time range. Updating one report does not affect the other reports displayed on the report page. When you create a real-time metrics report, it is displayed on the Real-time metrics page, and updates automatically to show current activity in your contact center.

Types of Real-time Metrics Reports

You can create the following types of real-time metrics reports in Amazon Connect.

Queues
Queues reports show contact data grouped by queue. For each contact that occurred during the report time range, the queue in which the contact was handled is displayed with metrics about Agent and Performance. When you create a Queues report, the first column in the report table is Queues, and the data in the table is data for the queue. You can view the routing profile associated with the queue by selecting the arrow next to the queue name.

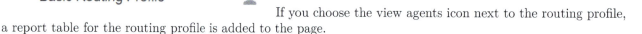
If you choose the view agents icon next to the routing profile, a report table for the routing profile is added to the page.

Agents
Agents reports show data about agents currently online in to your contact center, grouped by agent. Only agents with a status of **Online** are included. When you create an Agents report, the first column in the report is the **Agent Login**, which is the agent's user name used to log in to Amazon Connect. The data in the report includes metrics for **Agent**, **Phone**, and **Performance**.

Routing profiles
Routing Profiles reports display data about activity in your contact center grouped by routing profile, and includes metrics for Agents and Performance.

To create a real-time metrics report

1. Log in to your contact center using an account that has at least Access permission for Access metrics. The **QualityAnalyst** and **CallCenterManager** security profiles include this permission.

2. Choose **Metrics and Quality**, **Real-time metrics**.

3. Choose the report type to create, **Queues**, **Agents**, or **Routing profiles**.

4. Optionally, select the number of rows to include per page, **5**, **10**, **20**, or **50**.

5. Customize the report to provide the view of your contact center that you want. For more information, see Customize Real-time Metrics Reports.

For **Queues** and **Routing profiles** reports, the first row of the report is a summary of the activity included in the report. You can hide the report and display only the summary row by choosing the up or down arrow displayed near the top-right corner of the report table.

Customize Real-time Metrics Reports

You can customize real-time metrics report you create to get the view of your contact center that is the most meaningful for your organization. To customize your report, choose the cog icon near the top-right corner of the report table.

insert image

The following settings are common to all real-time metrics reports.

On the **Time Range** tab:

- Trailing windows for time the previous X hour(s)—select the time range, in hours, for data included in the report displayed on the Real-time metrics dashboard. You can select from the following values:
    - .5
    - 1
    - 2
    - 4
    - 8
    - 12
    - 24
- **Midnight to now**—display data for your contact center from midnight to the current time in the Time Zone selected. If you select a time zone other than the one you are currently in, the data reflects activity starting at midnight for the calendar day in that time zone, not your current time zone.

On the **Filters** tab:

- **Primary filter**—select whether to include all data from your contact center in the report tables, or include only the data for the specific items you select in the **Include** drop-down. You can select from the following filters:
    - **All**—data for all activity in your contact center is included in the report.

- **Queues**—when you select **Queues**, the queues in your contact center are displayed in the Include drop-down. You can select one or more queues to include in the report. Data for queues not selected is not included in the report.
- **Routing profiles**—when you select **Routing profiles**, you can filter data included in the report to include only data from the routing profiles you select in the Include drop-down.
- **Agent Hierarchies**—select which agent hierarchies to display data for in the report. This filter is available only for **Agents** reports.

On the **Metrics** tab:

Select the metrics to include in the report. The metrics available depend on the type of report.

- For **Queues** reports, metrics for **Agents** and **Performance** are included.
- For **Agents** reports, metrics for **Agent**, **Phone**, and **Performance** are included.
- For **Routing profiles** report, metrics for **Agents** and **Performance** are included.

For details about each metric, see Real-time Metrics Available in Amazon Connect.

Save a Real-time Metrics Report

When you create the report you want, you can save it so that you can access it in the future. Instead of customizing the default report template, you can just open the saved report to view it.

1. After you customize a report, choose **Save** or **Save As**.

   If you previously saved the report, when you choose **Save** the updated report is saved over the previous version.

2. If you choose **Save as**, or **Save** for a report that you have not saved previously, provide a name for your report.

3. Choose **Save** or **Save as**.

You can access the saved report from the **Saved reports** page by choosing **Metrics and Quality**, **Saved reports**, and then choose the **Real-time metrics** tab.

Download a Real-time Metrics Report as a .csv File

You can download the data included in your report as a comma-separated value (.csv) file so that you can use it with other applications. When you download the report, the fields included in the report are the same as the metrics you selected for the report. Metrics for which there is no data to include in the report show a dash in the downloaded .csv file.

1. Create and customize the report to download.

2. Choose the down arrow next to **Save** in the top-right corner of the page.

3. Choose **Download CSV**.

4. Confirm the action to take for the file in the browser dialog displayed.

Add a Report to the reports page

You can add multiple real-time metrics reports to the reports page to get different views of the activity in your contact center.

1. Create a Real-time metrics report.

2. On the **Real-time metrics** page, choose **New table**, and then the report type to add, **Queue, Routing profiles**, or **Agents**.

   A new report table is added to the page using the default report template.

3. Optionally, customize the report to get the view you want. Making changes to the added table does not affect the other tables already on the page.

Clear the Real-time metrics Page

If you want to create a new report page, you can remove all of the report tables you added to your page at once.

1. Choose the down arrow next to **Save** in the top-right corner of the page.

2. Choose **Clear**.

Real-time Metrics Available in Amazon Connect

The following sections describe the metrics available to include in real-time metrics reports in Amazon Connect. The metrics available to include in a report depend on the report type.

Metrics Available in Queues and Routing Profiles Reports

The following metrics are available to include in both **Queues** and **Routing profiles** real-time metrics reports.

Agents

The following agent metrics are included in default reports.

- **Online**—Number of agents with a status other than offline.
- **On call**—Number of agents currently active on a contact.
- **NPT**—Non-productive time (NPT) is the number of agents in a non-productive status, such as **Unavailable**.
- **ACW**—After call work (ACW) is the number of agents currently with a status of **After Call Work**.
- **Error**—Number of agents in an error status.
- **Available**—Number of agents with a status of **Available**.
- **Staffed**—Number of agents currently logged in and with a status of **Available, On call**, or in **ACW**.

Metrics Available in Performance Reports

The following performance metrics are included in default reports.

- **In queue**—Number of customers currently waiting in the queue.
- **Oldest**—Length of time in the queue for the contact that has been in the queue the longest.
- **Scheduled**—Number of customers for which there is a call back scheduled for this queue.
- **Queued**—Number of contacts currently in the queue.
- **Handled**—Number of contacts in this queue that were answered by an agent.
- **Abandoned**—Number of contacts that were abandoned from the queue during the reporting time range.
- **AHT**—Average handled time (AHT) is the average time, from start to finish, that a contact was connected with an agent. This is calculated by averaging the amount of time between the call being answered by an agent and the call ending.
- **SL 60**—SL refers to service level, and is the number of contacts that were in the queue for less than 60 seconds.

Additional Real-time Metrics Available for Reports

The following metrics are available to include in reports, but are not included in reports by default.

- **SL 15**—Number of contact that were in the queue for less than 15 seconds.
- **SL 20**—Number of contact that were in the queue for less than 20 seconds.
- **SL 25**—Number of contact that were in the queue for less than 25 seconds.
- **SL 30**—Number of contact that were in the queue for less than 30 seconds.
- **SL 45**—Number of contact that were in the queue for less than 45 seconds.
- **SL 90**—Number of contact that were in the queue for less than 90 seconds.
- **SL 120**—Number of contact that were in the queue for less than 120 seconds.
- **SL 180**—Number of contact that were in the queue for less than 180 seconds.
- **SL 240**—Number of contact that were in the queue for less than 240 seconds.
- **SL 300**—Number of contact that were in the queue for less than 300 seconds.
- **SL 600**—Number of contact that were in the queue for less than 600 seconds.
- **Agent hung up**—Number of contact in the queue that ended because the agent hung up before the customer.
- **Handled in**—Number of incoming contacts in the queue during the specified time range that were handled by an agent.
- **Handled out**—Number of outbound contacts in the queue during the specified time range that were handled by an agent.
- **Hold abandons**—Number of contact that disconnected while the customer was on hold. A disconnect could be because the customer hung up while on hold, or that there was a technical issue with the contact while on hold.
- **Consult**—Number of contacts in the queue that were handled by an agent, and the agent consulted with another agent or call center manager during the contact.
- **Max Queued**—The longest amount of time that a contact spent in the queue before being connected to an agent or hanging up the call before being connected to an agent. This includes any contact that was added to the queue, even if the contact was not connected with an agent, such as abandoned contacts.
- **Missed**—Number of contacts added to the queue but not answered by agents. This does not include abandoned contacts.
- **Avg abandon time**—Average amount of time, in seconds, that abandoned contacts were in the queue before being abandoned.
- **Avg queue answer time**—Average amount of time, in seconds, that a contact was in the queue before being answered by an agent. This is calculated using only the amount of time that the contact was in the queue, and not any time the contact spent in prior steps of the contact flow, such as listening or responding to prompts.
- **Avg hold time**—Average amount of time, in seconds, that a contact in the queue was on hold.
- **Avg interaction time**—Average amount of time, in seconds, that contacts were connected to and interacting with, agents. This does not include hold time or time spent waiting in a queue.
- **Avg interaction and hold time**—Average amount of time, in seconds, that contacts in the queue spent interacting with agents and on hold. This is the same as **Avg hold time** plus **Avg interaction time**.
- **Transferred in**—Number of contacts transferred in to the queue during the time range.
- **Transferred out**—Number of contacts transferred out from the queue during the time range.

Metrics Available in Agents Reports

The following metrics are available in Agents real-time metrics reports.

Agent Metrics

- **Agent Name**—the agent's name, displayed as last name, first name.
- ****Agent Last Name ****—the agent's last name as entered in their Amazon Connect user account.
- ****Agent First Name ****—the agent's first name as entered in their Amazon Connect user account.

- **Status**—the agent's current status, such as **Available** or **After Call Work**.
- **Duration**—the length of time that the agent has been in the current status.
- **Agent Hierarchy**—the hierarchy the agent is assigned to, if any.
- **Routing Profile**—the routing profile the agent is assigned to.

Phone Metrics

- **Active**—Displays 1 if the agent is currently active on call, otherwise shows 0.
- **Availability**—displays 1 if the agent is currently in Available status, otherwise shows 0.
- **Contact State**—shows the state of the most recent contact the agent handled, such as After Call Work.
- **Queue**—shows the name of the queue associated with the most recent contact the agent handled.

Performance Metrics

- **Avg ACW**—the average amount of time an agent spent in ACW status during the report time range.
- **Missed**—the number of calls missed by the agent during the time range.
- **Handled in**—the number of incoming contacts the agent handled during the time range.
- **Handled out**—the number of outgoing contacts the agent handled during the time range.
- **AHT**—the average amount of time the agent spent handling contacts during the time range.
- **Occupancy**—the per cent of time the agent was occupied during the report time range.

Historical Metrics Reports

Historical metrics reports include data about past, completed activity and performance in your contact center. You can generate the following reports for historical metrics in Amazon Connect.

- Queues
  - Contact metrics
  - Agent metrics
- Agents
  - Agent performance
  - Agent status
  - Agent activity audit
- Phone numbers
  - Contact metrics

The report selections use the same metrics, but group and order the data in the report a different way. Which fields that are included in a historical metrics report depends on the type of report and the grouping for the report.

You can customize the default report settings to get the view of the data that is most meaningful to you and your organization. You can change the time frame for the report, which metrics are included in the report, and how the data is grouped within the report.

About Custom Agent Statuses

You can create custom statuses for agents. These custom statuses are included only in some reports with some grouping options. For example, they are not included in **Queue Agent Metrics** reports that are grouped by queue.

Create a Historical Metrics Report

You can create historical metrics reports to view historical data for activity in your contact center.

1. Log in to your Amazon Connect instance.

2. Choose **Metrics and Quality**, **Historical metrics**.

3. Select the type of report to create.

   If you choose a **Queues**, **Agent performance**, or **Phone numbers**, the report is generated when you choose the report type.

4. To create **Agent status** or **Agent activity audit** reports, do one of the following:

   - Choose **Agent status**, then select the **Time Zone**, **Start date**, **End Date**, and **Filter By** value for the report, and then choose **Generate Report**.

     You can filter reports by **Agent** or **Routing Profile** in the **Filter by** drop-down menu.

   - Choose **Agent activity audit**, then select an agent in the **Agent Login** list and specify the **Date** and **Time Zone** to use for the report.

Add a Report to the Dashboard

You can add multiple real-time metrics reports to the dashboard to get different views of the activity in your contact center.

1. Create a Historical metrics report.

2. On the **Historical metrics** page, choose **New table**, and then the report type to add, **Queue**, **Routing profiles**, or **Agents**.

   A new report table is added to the page using the default report template.

3. Optionally, customize the report to get the view you want. Making changes to the added table does not affect the other tables already on the page.

Save a Historical Metrics Report

When you create the report you want, you can save it so that you can access it in the future. Instead of customizing the default report template, you can just open the saved report to view it.

1. After you customize a report, choose **Save** or **Save As**.

   If you previously saved the report, when you choose **Save** the updated report is saved over the previous version.

2. If you choose **Save as**, or **Save** for a report that you have not saved previously, provide a name for your report.

3. Choose **Save** or **Save as**.

You can access the saved report from the **Saved reports** page by choosing **Metrics and Quality, Saved reports**, and then choose the **Historical metrics** tab.

Download a Historical Metrics Report as a .csv File

You can download the data included in your report as a comma-separated value (.csv) file so that you can use it with other applications. When you download the report, the fields included in the report are the same as the metrics you selected for the report. Metrics for which there is no data to include in the report show a dash in the downloaded .csv file.

1. Create and customize the report to download.

2. Choose the down arrow next to **Save** in the top-right corner of the page.

3. Choose **Download CSV**.

4. Confirm the action to take for the file in the browser dialog displayed.

Clear the Historical Metrics Dashboard

If you want to create a new dashboard, you can remove all of the report tables you added to your dashboard at once.

1. Choose the down arrow next to **Save** in the top-right corner of the page.

2. Choose **Clear**.

Customize Historical Metrics Reports

When you change the settings for a report you have open, the report displayed on the page is updated to reflect the new settings, but those settings changes to not affect the default report displayed. You can save the changes to a new report, and then open that report from the Saved reports page. You can also set a schedule for the report to generate a report with your settings with the recurrence you define.

Note that scheduling a report also makes the report accessible by any other users in your Amazon Connect instance that have permissions to view Saved reports. Any user with sufficient permissions can also modify your scheduled report. Scheduled reports are saved as .csv files in the Amazon Simple Storage Service (Amazon S3) bucket defined for reports in your instance. You can choose to add a prefix to the report files sent to Amazon S3 on the **Delivery Options** tab of the **Schedule Report** settings.

Important
For scheduled reports, there is a delay of 15 minutes after the scheduled report time before the report is generated. This is to ensure that the report includes all of the data about activity that occurred during the time range specified for the report. Data from your contact center is not immediately processed and available to include in reports, so some data from the time range may not be captured in a report if the report is generated at the second the time range ends. For example, if you create a scheduled report for time frame of 8:00 AM to 5:00 PM, and there is activity in your contact center between 4:46:00 PM and 4:59:59 PM, the data about that activity may not be aggregated prior 5:00 PM when the report is scheduled to generate. Instead, the report is generated after 5:15 PM, by which time the data for the last 15 minutes of the time range is included in the report.

Table Settings

To change the setting for a historical metrics report, choose the cog icon near the top-right corner of the report page.

You can change the following settings when you create a historical metrics report:

Interval & Time Range

Specify values for the following settings for your report:

- **Interval**—Choose the interval for displaying data in the report **30 Minutes**, **Daily**, or **Total**. If you select **30 Minutes**, the report is displayed with a row of data for each 30 minute period during the time range for the report. When you select **Daily**, the report includes a row for each day in the time range per grouping option, such as queue. When you select **Total**, all of the data for the entire time range is displayed as a single row on the report.

- **Time range**—select the time range for data to include in the report. When the report is exported to your Amazon S3 bucket, the file name for the exported file includes the date and the UTC time at which the report was created. The **Last modified date** for the file is displayed using the time zone for the Amazon S3 bucket, and may not match the creation time for the report in UTC time. When you choose a time range, the hour at which a day starts is determined by the time zone selected. Reports default to UTC for the time zone. To generate reports that match your calendar days, select the time zone for your area, or the region in which you created your instance.

  The selections available for the **Time range** depend on the **Interval** you select. You can choose from the following values:

  - **Today (since 12 am)**—include metrics for the current calendar day starting at 12 AM in the selected time zone.
  - **Last 24 hours**—Displays data for the previous 24 hours from the current time.
  - **Yesterday**—include metrics for the previous calendar day, determined by the time zone selected.
  - **Last 2 days**—include metrics for the previous 2 calendar days, determined by the selected time zone. The report does not include data from the current day.
  - **Last 3 days**—include metrics for the previous 3 calendar days, determined by the selected time zone. The report does not include data from the current day.
  - **Last 7 days**—include metrics for the previous 7 calendar days, determined by the selected time zone. The report does not include data from the current day.
  - **Last week (Sun – Sat)**—include metrics for the previous calendar week, from Sunday at 12:00:00 AM to Saturday at 11:59:59 PM. The final second of the day is included in the data included in the report.
  - **Month to date**—include metrics for the days in the current calendar month up to 12:00:00 AM the current day. Metrics from the current day, which starts at midnight in the selected time zone, are not included.
  - **Last 30 days**—include metrics from the previous 30 calendar days, determined by the time zone selected. Data for the current day is not included in the report.
  - **Previous month**—include metrics for the previous calendar month, determined by the time zone selected.
  - **Custom time range**—choose a custom time range for the report.

- **Time Zone**—Select the time zone to use for the report. The time zone you choose is important, as the start and end of a calendar day is determined by the time zone you choose. If your local time is in a different time zone than the time zone selected for reports, the report uses 12:00:00 AM in the time zone selected, and not the time zone you are in. For example, if your organization uses times in the US-Pacific time zone, UTC-8, the calendar day starts 8 hours after midnight UTC time, or 4 PM local time. If you use UTC for the time zone for reports, the calendar day for the report is from 4 PM to 4 PM in your time zone rather than 12:00 AM to 12:00 AM. If your agents are staffed for shifts that end at 5 PM, your daily report includes agent metrics data for their shift until 4 PM local time. The remaining hour between 4 PM to 5 PM is included in the next calendar day when UTC time is selected for the report.

  You should use the same time zone for reports over time to get accurate and consistent metrics data for your contact center. Using different time zones for different reports may result in different data for the same time range selection.

Groupings

You can select from the following settings for grouping, or organizing, data in the report.

- **Grouping options**—choose the + next to an option to move it to the **Selected groupings** column. Report data is displayed in the report grouped by the fields in the **Selected groupings** column. For example, if you select Total for a time interval, and select **Queue** as the grouping option, the queue name is displayed as the first column in the report. If you select a time interval other than Total, the time interval is displayed as the first column in the report.

  Report data, such as average times and contacts handled, reflect the values for the queue under which they are grouped. If you choose **Agent** as the grouping option, the first column in the report is the agent name, and the data in the report reflects averages and contacts handled for each agent across all queues and routing profiles. The metrics you include on a report can be grouped in different ways to provide greater insight into how your contact center is performing.

  You can group reports on the following:

  - **Agent**
  - **Agent Hierarchy Level One**
  - **Agent Hierarchy Level Two**
  - **Agent Hierarchy Level Three**
  - **Agent Hierarchy Level Four**
  - **Agent Hierarchy Level Five**
  - **Phone Number**
  - **Queue**

  You can select only one agent hierarchy at a time for grouping. If you have not defined any agent hierarchies, the grouping option is greyed out and not selectable.

- **Selected groupings (Maximum 5)**—you can choose to group report data by up to 5 of the available grouping options. When only one grouping option is selected, all report data is grouped by that option. When more than one option is selected, report data is first grouped by the grouping option that is first in the list, and then those records are grouped within that group by the additional grouping option added to the **Selected groupings** column.

Understanding How Grouping Affects Historical Metrics Calculations

When you create a report, the values for calculated metrics are displayed as rows in the report. The rows in the report are grouped by the grouping option you select. The grouping of the data allows you to generate global data for your contact center, or more specific data for queues, agents, routing profiles, or agent hierarchy defined in your contact center. The metric calculations, and therefore metrics values displayed in the report, are different when reports are grouped differently. If you group the report results by queue, the value displayed for a metric is inclusive of all contacts associated with the queue.

For example, consider the **Contacts handled** metric. This metric is a count of the contacts handled during the time range defined for the report. With the default grouping, **Queue**, the value for **Contacts handled** is the total number of contacts handled during the time range from that queue by all agents in your contact center.

- If you group the report by **Agent**, the **Contacts handled** metric is the total number of contacts handled by the agent during the time range across all queues and routing profiles.
- If you group the report by routing profile, only contacts handled by agents assigned the routing profile and included in the count of contacts handled.
- If you group the report by queue, then agent, then routing profile, the value for **Contacts handled** is the total number of contacts an agent that is assigned the routing profile handled from the queue.

Agent activity can be included in one routing profile at a time, but agents can switch between routing profiles over the reporting time interval. If agents are assigned multiple routing profiles and handle contacts from multiple queues, there are multiple rows in the report for each routing profile assigned to the agent and the queue that the agent handled contacts from.

How Metrics Data Differs by Report Type

When you generate a report, the values displayed for each metric may be different for each report type or grouping option you choose. Some grouping options are more meaningful for some report types than for others. If you group a report by agent, the values for metrics associated with queues may not provide much insight. For some reports, you cannot add some metrics, select some grouping options, or use some filters. For example:

- When you group a report by queue, the metric values displayed reflect data for the metric grouped for the queue during the specified time range. If you look at the value for the Average Customer Hold time, it shows the average amount of time that customers spent on hold for each queue.
- When you group the report by agent, the metric values displayed reflect data for the metric grouped by agent. The value for Average customer hold time shows the average time for each agent across all queues to which the agent is assigned.
- When the report is grouped by Routing profile, the report shows the value for metrics grouped by routing profile, so will show Average Customer hold time by routing profile.

You can customize the metrics reports to get the view of your contact center that makes the most sense for your organization.

Filters

You can select filters for your report to limit the data included in a report to a specific category, such as queue or routing profile. When you select filters, the numbers of filters you selected is displayed next to the filter category. The fields available to select for filtering depends on the grouping selected for a report.

You must select at least one metric for a report. An exclamation point (!) is displayed next to any metrics displayed next to metrics that are not available to include in the report with the selected grouping.

You can filter on the following categories:

- **Queue**—Select one or more queues for which you want to include data in the report. If you do not select any queues, all queues are included in the report. You can search for a queue by typing the name of the queue in the Search field, or scroll through the queues listed in the drop-down list, and then select the check box to filter the report results to that queue.
- **Routing profile**—Select one or more routing profiles for which you want to filter data in the report. When you choose a routing profile, data is displayed only for the agents that are assigned that routing profile. If you do not select any routing profiles, agent data for all routing profiles is included in the report. To select a routing profile, type the name of the profile in the Search box, or scroll through the drop-down list. Select the check box next to one or more profiles to filter results in the report.
- **Agent hierarchy**—Select one or more agent hierarchies to filter data in the report to contacts handled by agents in the selected hierarchy. If you do not select a hierarchy, data for all contacts handled by agents in all hierarchies is included in the report. When only one hierarchy is selected, you can select a more granular filter within the hierarchy.
- **Phone number**—Select one or more phone numbers for your contact center to filter report data to include only contacts associated with the phone number or numbers selected. If you do not select a phone number, data for contacts on all phone numbers is included in the report.

Clear a Selected Filter

If you want to remove one of the filters you selected for a report, you can either deselect the check box next to the filter in the drop-down list, or choose the x next to the filter name displayed below the **Search** field on the **Filters** tab.

Metrics

Choose the metrics or fields to include in the report. Only the metrics you select are displayed in the report and included in report data stored in Amazon S3. The selections you make do not affect which metrics are calculated, generated, and included in contact trace records. To see different data for a time range, you can create another report and use different filters or groupings without affecting other reports or the default reports in Amazon Connect. The definitions for each metric are included in the following section.

Historical Metrics Definitions

The following metrics are available to include in historical metrics reports in Amazon Connect.

Agent Name
The agent's name, displayed as Last name, First name.

Agent First Name
The agent's first name as entered in their Amazon Connect user account.

Agent Last Name
The agent's last name as entered in their Amazon Connect user account.

After contact work time
Sum of the amount of time spent in After Contact Work (ACW) status after handling contacts. Agents enter ACW status after they end a call with a customer. ACW status ends when the agent changes to a different status.
You can specify an After call work timeout value in user profiles.

Agent on contact time
Sum of time that an agent was on a contact, including hold time and after call work. Most of the time, this is calculated with the following formula:
`Agent on Contact time = AgentInteractionDuration + CustomerHoldDuration + After contact work time` (including callbacks).
In some cases, the value reported for this metric also includes agent time spent in an auxiliary state. The time in the auxiliary state is included in the metric value, but not available in the CTR or as a separate metric.

Agent idle time
Sum of time that an agent spent in a productive status, but not handling contacts. A productive status is any status other than **Offline** or any custom agent status that you create.

Non-Productive Time
Amount of time agents spent in a status other than Error or Offline, but was not handling contacts.

Average queue abandon time
Average amount of time that customers spent in a queue before abandoning the call. This is calculated by averaging the difference between the EnqueueTimestamp and DequeueTimestamp for contacts that were abandoned while in a queue. Any call that was placed in a queue but not picked up by an agent or transferred to a callback is considered an abandoned call.

Average after contact work time
Average time that an agent spent in After contact work time status. This is calculated by averaging the **AfterContactWorkDuration** for all contacts included in the report based on the selected filters.

Average queue answer time
Average of time that contacts were in a queue before being answered by an agent. This is the average for `QueueInfo:Duration`.

Average handle time
Average of **Contact handle time** for all contacts handled by the agent. **Contact handle time** is the time an agent spent on a contact, including after call work.

Average customer hold time
The average of `CustomerHoldDuration` (from the CTR), which is time customers spent on hold after being connected to an agent.

Average agent interaction and customer hold time
Average of the sum of agent interaction and customer hold time. This is calculated by averaging the sum of `AgentInteractionDuration` plus `CustomerHoldDuration`.

Average agent interaction time
Average amount of time that agents interacted with customers on contacts.

Contacts abandoned
Number of contacts when the customer disconnected while waiting in a queue before being connected to an agent. Calls that transfer to callbacks are not counted as abandoned.

Contacts abandoned in 15 seconds
Count of contacts when the customer disconnected while in the queue for less than 15 seconds.

Contacts abandoned in 20 seconds
Count of contacts when the customer disconnected while in the queue for less than 20 seconds.

Contacts abandoned in 25 seconds
Count of contacts when the customer disconnected while in the queue for less than 25 seconds.

Contacts abandoned in 30 seconds
Count of contacts when the customer disconnected while in the queue for less than 30 seconds.

Contacts abandoned in 45 seconds
Count of contacts when the customer disconnected while in the queue for less than 45 seconds.

Contacts abandoned in 60 seconds
Count of contacts when the customer disconnected while in the queue for less than 60 seconds.

Contacts abandoned in 90 seconds
Count of contacts when the customer disconnected while in the queue for less than 90 seconds.

Contacts abandoned in 120 seconds
Count of contacts when the customer disconnected while in the queue for less than 120 seconds.

Contacts abandoned in 180 seconds
Count of contacts when the customer disconnected while in the queue for less than 180 seconds.

Contacts abandoned in 240 seconds
Count of contacts when the customer disconnected while in the queue for less than 240 seconds.

Contacts abandoned in 300 seconds
Count of contacts when the customer disconnected while in the queue for less than 300 seconds.

Contacts abandoned in 600 seconds
Count of contacts when the customer disconnected while in the queue for less than 600 seconds.

Contacts agent hung up first
Count of contacts when the agent disconnected before the customer.

Contacts consulted
Count of contacts when an agent consulted with a third party. The agent interacts with the third party, but the customer is not transferred to the third party.

Contacts handled
Count of contacts handled by an agent, including both incoming and outgoing contacts.

Contacts handled incoming
Count of incoming contacts handled by an agent.

Contacts handled outbound
Count of outbound contacts that were handled by an agent. This includes contacts that were initiated using the StartOutboundVoiceContact operation in the Amazon Connect API.

Contacts put on hold
Count of contacts put on hold by an agent one or more times.

Contacts hold disconnect
Count of contacts disconnected while the customer was on hold. This includes both the agent and the customer ending the contact.

Contacts hold agent disconnect
Count of contacts that were disconnected by the customer while the customer was on hold.

Contacts incoming
Count of incoming contacts to the contact center. This is the count of contact that initiated outside of Amazon Connect, not contacts that start in Amazon Connect and go out to customers.

Contacts answered in 15 seconds
Count of contacts that were answered by an agent within 15 seconds of being placed in a queue, based on the EnqueueTimestamp.

Contacts answered in 20 seconds
Count of contacts that were answered by an agent within 20 seconds of being placed in a queue, based on the EnqueueTimestamp.

Contacts answered in 25 seconds
Count of contacts that were answered by an agent within 25 seconds of being placed in a queue, based on the EnqueueTimestamp.

Contacts answered in 30 seconds
Count of contacts that were answered by an agent within 30 seconds of being placed in a queue, based on the EnqueueTimestamp.

Contacts answered in 45 seconds
Count of contacts that were answered by an agent within 45 seconds of being placed in a queue, based on the EnqueueTimestamp.

Contacts answered in 60 seconds
Count of contacts that were answered by an agent within 60 seconds of being placed in a queue, based on the EnqueueTimestamp.

Contacts answered in 90 seconds
Count of contacts that were answered by an agent within 90 seconds of being placed in a queue, based on the EnqueueTimestamp.

Contacts answered in 120 seconds
Count of contacts that were answered by an agent within 120 seconds of being placed in a queue, based on the EnqueueTimestamp.

Contacts answered in 180 seconds
Count of contacts that were answered by an agent within 180 seconds of being placed in a queue, based on the EnqueueTimestamp.

Contacts answered in 240 seconds
Count of contacts that were answered by an agent within 240 seconds of being placed in a queue, based on the EnqueueTimestamp.

Contacts answered in 300 seconds
Count of contacts that were answered by an agent within 300 seconds of being placed in a queue, based on the EnqueueTimestamp.

Contacts answered in 600 seconds
Count of contacts that were answered by an agent within 600 seconds of being placed in a queue, based on the `EnqueueTimestamp`.

Contacts queued
Count of contacts placed into a queue.

Contacts transferred in
Count of contacts transferred to a queue by an agent.

Contacts transferred out
Count of contacts transferred out of a queue after being answered by an agent.

Contacts transferred out internal
Count of contacts for the queue that were transferred by an agent to an internal source, such as a queue or another agent. An internal source is any source that can be added as a Quick Connect.

Contacts transferred out external
Count of contact for the queue that were transferred to an external source, such as a phone number that is external to your contact center.

Error status time
Sum of time that an agent spent in the **Error** status.

Customer hold time
Sum of the time that customers spent on hold after being connected to an agent. This includes time spent on a hold when being transferred, but does not include time spent in a queue.

Agent answer rate
Percentage of contacts routed to an agent that were successfully answered. Calculated by the following:
`(Contacts Handled / Contacts Routed)* 100`

Maximum queued time
The longest amount of time that a customer spent waiting in a queue during the time interval for the report.

Contacts missed
Count of the contacts missed. A contact is considered missed when it is routed to an agent but the agent did not accept the call for any reason. The same contact may be counted as missed multiple times, once for each time it is routed to an agent but then not picked up by an agent.

Contact handle time
Sum of time that an agent spent on contacts, including hold time and **After contact work time**.

Contact flow time
The time a contact spent in a contact flow.
Outbound contacts do not start in a contact flow, so outbound contacts are not included in the metric.

Occupancy
The percentage of time that agents were active on contacts. This is calculated by:
`Agent Handle Time/(Agent Handle Time + Agent Idle Time)`

Service level 15 seconds
Percentage of contacts answered within 15 seconds after being placed in a queue, based on the **EnqueueTimeStamp**.

Service level 20 seconds
Percentage of contacts answered within 20 seconds after being placed in a queue, based on the **EnqueueTimeStamp**.

Service level 25 seconds
Percentage of contacts answered within 25 seconds after being placed in a queue, based on the **EnqueueTimeStamp**.

Service level 30 seconds
Percentage of contacts answered within 30 seconds after being placed in a queue, based on the **EnqueueTimeStamp**.

Service level 45 seconds
Percentage of contacts answered within 45 seconds after being placed in a queue, based on the **EnqueueTimeStamp**.

Service level 60 seconds
Percentage of contacts answered within 60 seconds after being placed in a queue, based on the **EnqueueTimeStamp**.

Service level 90 seconds
Percentage of contacts answered within 90 seconds after being placed in a queue, based on the **EnqueueTimeStamp**.

Service level 120 seconds
Percentage of contacts answered within 120 seconds after being placed in a queue, based on the **EnqueueTimeStamp**.

Service level 180 seconds
Percentage of contacts answered within 180 seconds after being placed in a queue, based on the **EnqueueTimeStamp**.

Service level 240 seconds
Percentage of contacts answered within 240 seconds after being placed in a queue, based on the **EnqueueTimeStamp**.

Service level 300 seconds
Percentage of contacts answered within 300 seconds after being placed in a queue, based on the **EnqueueTimeStamp**.

Service level 600 seconds
Percentage of contacts answered within 600 seconds after being placed in a queue, based on the **EnqueueTimeStamp**.

Online time
Sum of the time that an agent spent in a status other than Offline. The time that an agent spends in any custom status you define for your instance is considered online, non-productive time.

Agent interaction and hold time
Sum of **Agent interaction time + Customer hold time**.

Agent interaction time
Sum of the time that agents spent interacting with customers. For calls, this is the amount of time agents spent talking to customers on the call.

Average outbound agent interaction time
Average time agents spent interacting with a customer during an outbound contact.

Average outbound after contact work time
Average time that agents spent in ACW status after outbound contacts.

Contact Trace Records Data Model

This document describes the data model for Amazon Connect contact trace records. Contact trace records capture the events associated with a contact in your Amazon Connect instance. Real-time and historical metrics are based on the data captured in contact trace records. To learn more about contact trace records and metrics in Amazon Connect, see Amazon Connect Metrics and Reports.

Endpoint

Information about an endpoint. In Amazon Connect, an endpoint is the destination for a contact, such as a customer phone number, or a phone number for your instance.

Type
The endpoint type. Currently, an endpoint can only be a telephone number.
Valid values: `TELEPHONE_NUMBER`

Address
The value for the type of endpoint. For TELEPHONE_NUMBER, the value is a phone number in E.164 format.
Type: String
Length: 1-256

AgentHierarchyGroup

Information about an agent hierarchy group.

ARN
The Amazon Resource Name (ARN) of the group.
Type: ARN

GroupName
The name of the hierarchy group.
Type: String
Length: 1-256

AgentHierarchyGroups

Information about the agent hierarchy. Hierarchies can be configured with up to five levels.

Level1
The group at level one of the agent hierarchy.
Type: AgentHierarchyGroup

Level2
The group at level two of the agent hierarchy.
Type: AgentHierarchyGroup

Level3
The group at level three of the agent hierarchy.
Type: AgentHierarchyGroup

Level4
The group at level four of the agent hierarchy.
Type: AgentHierarchyGroup

Level5
The group at level five of the agent hierarchy.
Type: AgentHierarchyGroup

QueueInfo

Information about a queue.

ARN
The Amazon Resource Name of the queue.
Type: ARN

Name
The name of the queue.
Type: String
Length: 1-256

EnqueueTimestamp
The date and time the contact was added to the queue.
Type: String (*yyyy-mm-dd*T*hh:mm:ss*Z)

DequeueTimestamp
The date and time the contact was removed from the queue. Either the customer disconnected or the contact was connected to an agent.
Type: String (*yyyy-mm-dd*T*hh:mm:ss*Z)

Duration
The difference in time, in whole seconds, between `EnqueueTimestamp` and `DequeueTimestamp`.
Type: Integer
Min value: 0

RoutingProfile

Information about a routing profile.

ARN
The Amazon Resource Name of the routing profile.
Type: ARN

Name
The name of the routing profile.
Type: String
Length: 1-100

RecordingInfo

Information about a recording.

Type
The recording type.
Valid values: `AUDIO`

Status
The recording status.
Valid values: `AVAILABLE` | `DELETED`

Location
The location, in Amazon S3, for the recording.
Type: String
Length: 0-256

DeletionReason
If the recording was deleted, this is the reason entered for the deletion.
Type: String

Agent

Information about the agent that handled the contact.

ARN
The Amazon Resource Name of the agent.
Type: ARN

Username
The username of the agent.
Type: String
Length: 1-100

HierarchyGroups
The agent hierarchy groups for the agent.
Type: AgentHierarchyGroups

RoutingProfile
The routing profile of the agent.
Type: RoutingProfile

ConnectedToAgentTimestamp
The date and time the contact was connected to the agent.
Type: String ($yyyy\text{-}mm\text{-}dd\text{T}hh\text{:}mm\text{:}ss\text{Z}$)

AgentInteractionDuration
The time, in whole seconds, that the agent talked with the customer.
Type: Integer
Min value: 0

CustomerHoldDuration
The time, in whole seconds, that the customer spent on hold while connected to the agent.
Type: Integer
Min value: 0

NumberOfHolds
The number of times the customer was put on hold while connected to the agent.
Type: Integer
Min value: 0

LongestHoldDuration
The longest time, in whole seconds, that the customer was put on hold by the agent.
Type: Integer
Min value: 0

AfterContactWorkStartTimestamp
The date and time the agent entered the After Contact Work status.
Type: String ($yyyy\text{-}mm\text{-}dd\text{T}hh\text{:}mm\text{:}ss\text{Z}$)

AfterContactWorkEndTimestamp
The date and time the agent left the After Contact Work status.
Type: String (*yyyy-mm-dd*T*hh:mm:ss*Z)

AfterContactWorkDuration
The difference in time, in whole seconds, between `AfterContactWorkStartTimestamp` and `AfterContactWorkEndTimestamp`.
Type: Integer
Min value: 0

ContactTraceRecord

Information about a contact.

AWSContactTraceRecordFormatVersion
The record format version.
Type: String

AWSAccountId
The ID of the AWS account that owns the contact.
Type: String

InstanceARN
The Amazon Resource Name of the instance.
Type: ARN

ContactId
The ID of the contact.
Type: String
Length: 1-256

InitialContactId
If this contact is related to other contacts, this is the ID of the initial contact.
Type: String
Length: 1-256

PreviousContactId
If this contact is not the first contact, this is the ID of the previous contact.
Type: String
Length: 1-256

NextContactId
If this contact is not the last contact, this is the ID of the next contact.
Type: String
Length: 1-256

Channel
The contact channel.
Valid values: VOICE

InitiationMethod
Indicates how the contact was initiated.
Valid values: `INBOUND` | `OUTBOUND` | `TRANSFER` | `CALLBACK` | `API`

InitiationTimestamp
The date and time this contact was initiated. For `INBOUND`, this is when the call arrived. For `OUTBOUND` and `CALLBACK`, this is when the agent began dialing. For `API`, this is when the request arrived.
Type: String (*yyyy-mm-dd*T*hh:mm:ss*Z)

ConnectedToSystemTimestamp
The date and time the customer endpoint connected to Amazon Connect. For `INBOUND`, this matches `InitiationTimestamp`. For `OUTBOUND`, `CALLBACK`, and `API`, this is when the customer endpoint answers.
Type: String (*yyyy-mm-dd*T*hh*:*mm*:*ss*Z)

TransferCompletedTimestamp
If this contact was transferred out of Amazon Connect, the date and time the transfer endpoint was connected.
Type: String (*yyyy-mm-dd*T*hh*:*mm*:*ss*Z)

TransferredToEndpoint
If this contact was transferred out of Amazon Connect, the transfer endpoint.
Type: Endpoint

DisconnectTimestamp
The date and time that the customer endpoint disconnected from Amazon Connect.
Type: String (*yyyy-mm-dd*T*hh*:*mm*:*ss*Z)

CustomerEndpoint
The customer endpoint.
Type: Endpoint

SystemEndpoint
The system endpoint. For `INBOUND`, this is the phone number that the customer dialed. For `OUTBOUND`, this is the caller ID phone number that Amazon Connect used to dial the customer.
Type: Endpoint

Queue
If this contact was queued, this is information about the queue.
Type: QueueInfo

AgentConnectionAttempts
The number of times Amazon Connect attempted to connect this contact with an agent.
Type: Integer
Min value: 0

Agent
If this contact successfully connected to an agent, this is information about the agent.
Type: Agent

Recording
If recording was enabled, this is information about the recording.
Type: RecordingInfo

Attributes
The contact attributes, formatted as a map of keys and values.
Type: Attributes
Members: `AttributeName`, `AttributeValue`

LastUpdateTimestamp
The date and time this contact was last updated.
Type: String (*yyyy-mm-dd*T*hh*:*mm*:*ss*Z)

Using the Amazon Connect Contact Control Panel

The Amazon Connect Contact Control Panel (CCP) is used by agents to communicate with contacts. The CCP can be used with a softphone or a desktop phone. The phone number and configurations are managed in Amazon Connect.

Amazon Connect CCP Concepts

Amazon Connect provides a number of management and configuration options for your contact center. The terminology and concepts that are central to your understanding and use of Amazon Connect are described below.

agent
Users who handle contacts using Amazon Connect.

softphone
A browser-based telephony service that is not linked to a handset. It can be used remotely, provided that the agent is logged in to Amazon Connect.

desk phone/handset
A physical telephone requiring an agent to be in its proximity in order to make or receive calls.

status
Metrics are gathered based on changes in agent status (available, offline, and so on).

after contact work
A state where the agent is no longer on a call but has related work to complete before being able to accept or make other calls.

leave
Leave a multi-party call without disconnecting the other parties or hanging up the call.

Launch the Amazon Connect CCP

You can log in to the CCP using the link provided by the Amazon Connect administrator. We recommend that you bookmark the URL for easy access. After you are logged in, choose the phone icon to open the CCP.

Set up Users and Permissions

Before agents can use the CCP to take calls, you configure permissions. These permissions are edited in Amazon Connect, and cover a range of activities from generating reports to making calls. The permissions also ensure that agents only see, and have access to, what's relevant to their job. For more information, see Managing User Profiles and Permissions.

Make International Calls

Making international calls using Amazon Connect is possible and the CCP provides the correct formatting for this automatically.

E.164 defines a general format for international telephone numbers. Numbers are limited to a maximum of 15 digits, excluding the international call prefix. The presentation of a number is usually prefixed with the plus sign (+), indicating that the number includes the country calling code. When dialing, the number must typically be prefixed with the appropriate international call prefix (in place of the plus sign), which is a trunk code to reach an international circuit from within the country of call origination. Phone numbers that are not formatted in E.164 may work, but it depends on the phone or handset that is being used as well as the carrier from which the call is being originated.

To express a US phone number to E.164 format, add the '+' prefix and the country code (1) in front of the number. In the UK and many other countries internationally, local dialing requires the addition of a 0 in front of the subscriber number. However, to use E.164 formatting, this 0 must be removed. A number such as 020 718 xxxxx in the UK would be formatted as +44 20 718 xxxxx.

Set up Softphones and Desk Phones

Before agents can use the CCP, check the following configurations:

- **Headset connectivity**—Check the settings in Device Management to ensure that your computer recognizes the headset and allows proper headset connectivity.
- **Set up headset**—You may need to adjust your browser settings to ensure correct peripheral selection.
- **Desktop notifications**—Ensure that the browser is not in incognito mode so that desktop notifications can be displayed.
- **Microphone**—Ensure that the microphone settings are always enabled.
- **Dialing**—In **Settings**, you can configure the softphone to dial a DID desk phone if required. When you choose a desk phone, enter the DID number to which calls go.

Softphone CCP IP Address Ranges

Agents can log in using the URL, user name, and password provided by their Amazon Connect administrator. Each agent has a unique user name and password.

If agents are using a softphone, the IP address used must be in the IP address range for the region where you created your Amazon Connect instance. The IP addresses used by Amazon Connect in each region are listed, along with the addresses for all AWS services, in the https://ip-ranges.amazonaws.com/ip-ranges.json file with the service name AMAZON_CONNECT.

You should allow UDP traffic on port 3478 for all addresses listed for the region in which you created your instance.

For more information, see AWS IP Address Ranges in the Amazon Web Services General Reference.

For agents to use the CCP, you also need to allow access for the softphone signaling endpoints, which are hosted in Amazon EC2.

When there are new IP address ranges supported for Amazon Connect, they are added to the publicly available ip-ranges.json for a minimum of 30 days before they are used by the service. After 30 days, softphone traffic through the new IP address ranges increases over the subsequent two weeks. After two weeks, traffic is routed through the new ranges equivalent to all available ranges.

Status Settings

The status settings are used for reporting purposes to ensure that system issues are resolved quickly and to manage resources.

The following settings are available:

- **Available**—Indicates that an agent is available to take calls.
- **Offline**—Logs agents out and removes them from the pool of available agents.

Work with Calls

Using the Contact Control Panel (CCP), you can perform the following actions on a softphone. When you opt for a desk phone, you have the same controls as softphone. The only difference is that there is no **Accept** button on a desk phone.

Accepting incoming calls

- To accept an incoming call, choose **Accept call**.
- To edit settings, choose **Settings**.
- To end a call, choose **End call**.
- To put a call on hold, choose **Hold**.

When a call is connected, a new set of options become available in the CCP.

Transfers

After an agent picks up a call, the agent can transfer the call by choosing the **Transfer** button and then choosing one of the available contacts. The contacts displayed are the quick connects defined in your Amazon Connect instance, which have been added to a queue in the agent's routing profile and are associated with a contact flow that support call transfers.

Agents can also manually enter a phone number to transfer calls to by choosing **Dial number** after answering the call. The agent can enter a phone number using the keypad, and then choose **Transfer** to transfer the call. If agents regularly transfer calls to a specific phone number, you can create an **External** contact flow and use that phone number for the destination.

To enable agent call transfers

1. Create and publish a contact flow for the type of transfer to enable.

   - To enable transfers to another agent, create a **transfer to agent** contact flow.
   - To enable transfers to a queue, create a **transfer to queue** contact flow.
   - External transfers do not require a specific type of contact flow. **Note**
     You must publish your contact flows to make them active in your contact center.

2. Create a quick connect for the type of transfer to enable: **Agent**, **Queue**, or **External**.

   When you create the **Agent** or **Queue** quick connect, select a contact flow that matches the type of transfer to enable. **External** quick connects require only a phone number, and do not allow you to set a queue or contact flow.

   For more information about quick connects, see Creating Quick Connects.

3. Add the quick connect that you created to any queue used in a contact flow for which to enable call transfer, such as the queue used in the contact flow for incoming calls. The queue must be in the routing profile assigned to the agent who should be able to transfer calls. The quick connects are displayed in the list of contacts when an agent tries to transfer an active call.

To transfer calls to an agent or queue

1. After accepting a call in the CCP, choose **Transfer**.

2. Select the contact to whom to transfer the call, and then choose **Dial**.

   The call is placed on hold during the transfer.

3. After the call is answered by an agent, or sent to a queue, choose **Leave call** to disconnect from the call.

4. To use conference, swap, or hold:

   - To begin a conference call, choose **Join** to perform a soft transfer. To drop out of the call, choose **Leave**.
   - Choose **Swap** to switch between talking to a customer and the person to whom you're transferring the call.
   - Choose **Hold all** to put all parties on hold.

Some settings that are configured in Amazon Connect include setting agents to go into the `After call work` state after they are done with their call. Agents can also be configured to accept a call automatically, without having to choose **Accept**.

Granting Microphone Access

If you're experiencing problems with your microphone, you may need to grant microphone access in your browser.

For Google Chrome steps, see Use your camera and microphone in Chrome.

For Mozilla Firefox steps, see Permissions Manager.

Important

A change introduced in Google Chrome version 64 may result in issues with receiving calls if you are using an embedded Contact Control Panel (CCP) softphone using the Amazon Connect Streams library. If you are experiencing issues with your microphone when using Chrome version 64, you can resolve the issue by building and deploying the latest version of the Amazon Connect Streams API, following the steps under *Downloading Streams*.

You can also resolve the issue by using Firefox as your browser.

How to Enable Manager Listen-in

As a manager, you can listen in on active calls as your agents interact with your customers. Only users that are assigned the **Enable** permissions for **Manager listen in** can listen in on agent calls. The **CallCenterManager** security profile includes this permission, but not permission to access the CCP. You can add the permission for the CCP to the **CallCenterManager** profile, or also assign the **Agent** profile to an account that is already assigned the **CallCenterManager** profile.

Before you can use the listen-in feature, you need to enable call recording in your contact flows. The listen-in feature works only when call recording is enabled.

To enable manager listen-in

1. Log in to your Amazon Connect instance using an account that has permissions to edit contact flows.

2. Identify a call flow that handles customer contacts that you want to listen in on.

3. Choose **Routing, Contact flows**, and then choose the name of the contact flow to open it in the editor.

4. Add a **Set call recording behavior** block to the contact flow, select **Agent and Customer** under **Record**, and then choose **Save**.

   Call recording must be enabled before the call being connected to an agent. **Important**
   Make sure that the block has connections to the block before and after it in the contact flow.

5. Choose **Save and Publish** to publish the updated contact flow. Choose **Save and Publish** again to confirm that you want to overwrite the published version.

To listen in on agent calls

1. Log in to your Amazon Connect instance with a user account that is assigned the **CallCenterManager** security profile, or that is enabled for the **Manager listen in** permission.

2. Open the CCP by choosing the phone icon in the top-right corner of the screen.

3. Choose **Metrics and quality, Real-time metrics**.

4. On the **Real-time metrics** page, choose **Agents**.

   For any agent that is on a call, there is a headset icon next to the agent's login name. Choose the icon to start listening to the call.

When you are listening to call, the status in your contact control panel changes to **Monitoring**.

5. To stop listening to the call, choose **End call**.

When the agent ends the call, monitoring stops automatically.

Document History

The following table describes the additions and updates to the documentation.

- **Latest documentation update:**June 18, 2018

Change	Description	Date
Added content for contact attributes.	Published a new topic on contact attributes and new system metrics atrributes in Amazon Connect, including the new Get metrics block. For more information, see Amazon Connect Contact Attributes.	June 18, 2018
Replaced the content on metrics and reports with new content.	The previous metrics content was replaced with new content, including Real-time and Historical metrics reports and metric descriptions, working with reports, and the Contact Trace Record (CTR) data model. For more information, see Amazon Connect Metrics and Reports.	May 22, 2018
Updated the data model content for agent event streams.	Updated the agent event streams data model content to use a new format, and change HierarchyGroups to AgentHierarchyGroups. For more information, see Agent Event Streams Data Model.	April 20, 2018
Added additional IP ranges for softphones.	Updated the list of IP address ranges required for using the softphone in the CCP. For more information, see Set up Softphones and Desk Phones.	March 30, 2018
Added Manager listen-in	Added steps to configure and enable a manager to listen in on agent calls. For more information, see How to Enable Manager Listen-in.	December 10, 2017
Added information about using outbound caller ID	Added details about how outbound caller ID works, and why sometimes customers may not see the information that you provide. For more information, see Amazon Connect Concepts.	December 10, 2017

Change	Description	Date
Added information about agent call transfer	Added details about how to enable call transfers from an agent to another agent, to a queue, or to an external number. For more information, see Work with Calls.	December 10, 2017
Added Contact Flow Logs	Added content for the new Contact Flow Logs. For more information, see Contact Flow Logs.	November 16, 2017
Added Contact Flow Import/-Export	Added content for the new Contact Flow Import/Export. For more information, see Contact Flow Import/Export.	November 16, 2017
Added Agent Event Streams	Added content for the new Agent Event Streams. For more information, see Agent Event Streams.	November 16, 2017
Added Login/Logout Report	Added content about the new Login/Logout reports. For more information, see Login/Logout Reports.	November 1, 2017
Removed the Loop block type from Branch group	Removed the information about the Loop block from the Branch group because the Loop block was removed from the service.	October 27, 2017
Added IP addresses for softphones	Added IP address and port information for connecting to each region using a softphone client. For more information, see Set up Softphones and Desk Phones.	October 27, 2017
Initial release	Initial release of the Amazon Connect User Guide.	March 28, 2017